THE ORIGINAL YOUNG TURK

Stories and Life Lessons from an American Dream Come True

DOGAN UYGUR

ARCHWAY
PUBLISHING

Archway Publishing books may be ordered through booksellers or by contacting:

Archway Publishing
1663 Liberty Drive
Bloomington, IN 47403
www.archwaypublishing.com
1 (888) 242-5904

Because of the dynamic nature of the Internet, any web addresses or links contained in this book may have changed since publication and may no longer be valid. The views expressed in this work are solely those of the author and do not necessarily reflect the views of the publisher, and the publisher hereby disclaims any responsibility for them.

Any people depicted in stock imagery provided by Getty Images are models, and such images are being used for illustrative purposes only. Certain stock imagery © Getty Images.

ISBN: 978-1-4808-8660-5 (sc)
ISBN: 978-1-4808-8658-2 (hc)
ISBN: 978-1-4808-8659-9 (e)

Library of Congress Control Number: 2020902918

Print information available on the last page.

Archway Publishing rev. date: 02/20/2020

Everything Starts and Ends with You

For my mother, Nuriye, my brother, Ihsan, and my wife, Nukhet.

Contents

Foreword

MY DAD IS MY HERO, my North Star—I'm the person I am today because of him. He taught me how to treat people with decency. He taught me the value of hard work. Most importantly, he believed in me, teaching me that I could be anything if I set my mind to it. There is enormous power in the sense that you can accomplish whatever it is you set out to do. My dad gave me that power through his faith in me.

He was born in a small house in a small town in southeastern Turkey. The family had no electricity. He was literally born with no power. His family, of course, had no money. They didn't even have a refrigerator. Imagine that for a second. Non-stop, they had to make their own food—there was nowhere to store what they made. Food preparation was essentially a full-time job.

They had no clocks. To this day, my dad wakes up—like clockwork—whenever he wants to. It is a skill born out of the necessity of his childhood. Here's a story few Americans can relate to: As a child, my dad had to wake up in the middle of the night to get the donkeys ready to go to the fields before the sun rose. He didn't have a clock to wake him or even tell him what time it was when he did get up.

How in the world did that guy wind up running several businesses in Turkey and America? How did he live the American Dream? Let me tell you how—through sheer force of will and a mountain of hard work. That's the point of this book—to show you how he did it and to serve as a guide to you as he was to me. Imagine the force of his example as I was growing up. How do I know anything is possible? Because I saw my dad do the impossible right in front of my eyes.

It's a good thing I'm not the kind of guy who worries about measuring up to his father. What could I possibly accomplish that would measure up to his story, going from no money, no power, and no hope to the top of the world? He gave me such an enormous head start in the world by bringing me to America, providing me a world class education, and helping me to start my business. Now perhaps you're beginning to see why I owe him everything. But let's talk about the subtle gifts he's given me that arguably have made an even bigger difference.

There's one day I remember in particular when I was in the sixth or seventh grade. I got a 98 percent on a test. When I told my dad, he asked me, "Where is the other 2 percent?" Some might think that's putting too much pressure on a kid, but I never perceived it that way at all. When my dad expected the very best from me, it instilled in me the presumption that I was capable of it.

He always believed I could get 100 on every test. Think about the message that sends to a young kid: "Of course you're capable of being the best." His message conveyed tremendous strength to me. It's where I get my deep reservoir of confidence. It was born of a father who consistently believed in his son.

My father is the strongest man I've ever known, even though he's never been in a fight. Of course, he's human, so, figuratively, he's been knocked down often, like we all have. But that's not the sign of his strength. His strength is in how he always got back up. No one—nor any crisis— was going to keep my father down.

I remember well the story of a friend of his— supposedly a close friend. Turns out, this alleged friend basically defrauded him, leaving him in a precarious spot financially. In fact, it might well have ended my father's business, leaving us with no money almost immediately after moving to this country. What was his response? To curse the man? To blame the Gods? No, my dad went to work, literally, rolling up his sleeves and deciding that he would fight his way out of the mess honestly. He worked night and day to make sure that he pulled himself—and his family—back out of danger. And remember, throughout his life he operated without a safety net. If he crashed, there was no one to rescue us. Again, imagine a young boy seeing the power of that example—of a father so strong that nothing could ever knock him out, strong enough to always provide for his family. There is nothing stronger or more loving in the world.

I often talk about my dad's toughness, but you should also know how much he loved my mom, my sister, and me. While we were still living in Turkey, there was a tiny place by the water we'd visit over the summer. We stayed there with my grandparents, yet every day my dad would wake up early and drive all the way into the city for work, often returning late at night. But the sun set late during the summer, and we'd all wait on the beach for my dad to come home. When he did, he'd make sure to come out and play with us in the water. No matter how many hours he'd put in; no matter how long his commute; no matter how tired he was. My favorite memory in the world is having my dad throw me up in the air and catch me in the water as the sun was setting on those summer nights.

One time, a friend and I decided that we'd engage in a goofy experiment just to experience my dad's reaction. Since he's such a straightforward, logical guy, we wondered what he'd do if one day he woke up and there were orange cones surrounding his car. I know—it was a weird thought. I happened to have these cones in my car—we used them to play touch football in the park. So we positioned the cones carefully around his car. Then we waited until morning. I know what I'd do—I'd wonder why there were cones around my car, who put them there, and what their purpose was. I would then ask everyone in the house—and any neighbor I saw—if they knew what was up with the cones.

By the time we woke, Dad had already left for the day. Naturally, he left so early, I missed the punch line to my own lame joke. Anyway, we went out to the driveway and saw three or four smashed orange cones. My dad had simply driven over them. When he got home, I asked him why he didn't ask anyone about the cones and why he decided to just drive over them. He looked at me like

I'd just asked the dumbest question in the world (which perhaps I had). "I had to get to work," he said.

That's my dad in a nutshell. It reminds me of the fable of the Gordian knot. It was said that the man who could untie the knot would conquer Asia. Countless men came and tried to solve the puzzle, but no one could do it. Then Alexander the Great came upon the knot and cut it with his sword—and went on to conquer Asia. The knot was in his way, and he was in a hurry to conquer. My dad didn't have the luxury of untying knots—or picking up cones. He was on a mission to provide for his family. And no cone, no knot, nothing was going to stand in his way.

Beyond all of this, the most powerful example he set for me was his enduring decency. For years after we arrived in the States, he'd bring Turkish college students over to our house. Then he'd find them jobs and make sure they were managing in this new, unfamiliar country. He'd also help his friends from Turkey land jobs here. He didn't even have to know the people he was helping— he would help strangers find opportunity where there seemed to be none. And my dad considered it his moral obligation to help all of his friends' children to find their way in the world. He had to have been the most effective job placement service in East Brunswick, New Jersey.

And he never considered any of that extra work a choice. It was simply the right thing to do, the decent thing to do. Where would he be, he thought, if his uncle hadn't let him stay in their house while he got a college education in Istanbul? Though he'd earned himself a free spot at a university by scoring highly on his exams, he still wouldn't have been able to go if his uncle hadn't given him a room. Never could he have afforded to live in Istanbul were it not for the kindness of others. He paid that kindness forward as a matter of course.

Though he gave me so much, he also didn't hesitate—on rare, but memorable occasions—to give away what he'd given me earlier. When I was a teenager, I finally had a Commodore 64 computer, allowing me to play some rudimentary video games. My dad thought buying an Atari was splurging. At least with the Commodore 64, he figured, I also had a computer and might actually learn something. But it didn't last. After a year or so, he turned around and gave it away to his secretary's son. Naturally, I asked him why. "Because he needs it more than you do."

Then there was the day he gave away my skis to a young employee of his who'd come from Turkey to work in the United States. "Dad," I argued, "those skis have my name on them!" He told me that if you have your name on skis, that means you're doing well enough. Then he told me the other guy had nothing and would now learn how to ski.

By the way, that former employee of my father's is now a successful businessman in Turkey. And if he's reading this, I'd like my skis back. They're the ones that say "Cenk Uygur" on them.

During the summer, I'd work in construction in my dad's buildings. I started working for him at a young age—young enough that I'm afraid to write down how old I was in print. But working for dad was like a master class in business and decency. One day I overheard a conversation between my dad and one of his employees, a recovering alcoholic. He was a good guy, although capable of getting himself in trouble from time to time, and he was a consistently hard worker. In this case, the guy was telling my dad that he'd gotten into a little bit of trouble—probably a fight—and he'd lost his glasses. He had terrible eyesight, but he didn't have the money he needed for new glasses—$400 is the number I remember in my mind. I was certain my dad would refuse the request for help because the guy only had himself to blame for losing his glasses. And believe me, despite my dad's generosity, he was not the type of man who gave away money for no reason. Remember, an Atari was "splurging."

But my father said yes right away, writing him a check on the spot. Later I walked into his office. "Why did you give him the money for the glasses even though it was obviously his fault?" I asked. Dad answered instantly. To him, the answer was obvious. "Because he couldn't see."

My dad has helped me, and so many others, see as well. For that—and so much more—I owe him everything.

—Cenk Uygur
March, 2019

Acknowledgments

WRITING THIS BOOK WAS A herculean challenge for me, and I would never have been able to complete it if it weren't for the encouragement of my friends and family, especially my daughter, Sedef, my son, Cenk, and my wife, Nukhet. Without their suggestions and advice, I wouldn't have even put a pen to paper in the first place. I thank them from the bottom of my heart.

I would also like to thank my first landlady, Ms. Farachie, with whom I lived when I moved from Turkey to the US in 1961. I couldn't speak a word of English, but through her constant conversation, whether on purpose or not, she was vital to my learning the language, a major milestone in my life.

Veronica Panagiotou of Highland, New Jersey, was of great help early in my writing process, as she made up for my lack of typing skills and helped me record and transcribe stories, thoughts, and ideas that I later used in this book. I also greatly appreciate all of the editorial and writing support I received from Zach Gajewski.

Lastly, I owe my whole life's story to my brother, Dr. Ihsan Uygur, and my mother, Nuriye Uygur. Ihsan put me on the right path, which led me to my future. Without him my life would be entirely different. All of my success—in my education, work, and family—grew from his guidance.

My mother brought me into this world and instilled in me many of the values that I have gone on to pass down to my children. Her care, strength, and love were unmatched, and I believe she'd be proud of both Ihsan and I if she could see us today.

Introduction

IN FEBRUARY OF 2016, MY son, Cenk, asked if he could interview me for one of his many shows on TYT Network, a progressive online news network that he co-founded nearly twenty years ago starting with the flagship show *The Young Turks*. The network's YouTube channel now averages almost two hundred-fifty million views per month and has become an internationally recognized and celebrated voice in the progressive political community. Cenk has interviewed the likes of Larry King, Oliver Stone, and countless politicians and commentators— including former US president Jimmy Carter and former New York governor Mario Cuomo—so I figured I was in good company. Watching Cenk start, run, and grow TYT has been one of my proudest experiences as a father, and for him to care enough about my life and opinions to take the time to invite me on his show filled me with a joy that only a father can know.

During the interview I told him many stories of my life, from my youth in southern Turkey to my education in America, from my business ventures to how his mother and I met and were married. He'd heard many of these before, but not all of them—I've always had a knack for the occasional surprise. When I left the studio that evening, I thought over my experiences and how I had gotten to where I am today. I had some good laughs with Cenk that afternoon, and I had relished the opportunity to speak about what contributed to my success and my understanding of the world. And that, as they say, was pretty much that.

But then something happened that surprised both Cenk and I. Once the video was posted to YouTube it received a few thousand hits, not unlike many of the other videos on the TYT network. Then it reached 5,000, then 10,000, and before we realized what was happening, it had shot its way up to 100,000. Soon after, it hit 210,000 views and continues to be viewed daily.

Once in a while, I would take a look at the comments thread beneath the video to see what people thought of our little discussion. I hadn't expected such a response, with people commenting that the interview was "amazing," "epic," the "best TYT interview ever," and that it "should be shown to all young people." Of course, it's easy to let praise go to one's head, but the comment that struck me the strongest came from a young man who wrote that he was eighteen years old, working to begin the "long journey of immigrating to America." He stated that my life's story had been "inspirational and touching." It's been almost six decades since I first came to the US, looking to make my own way in the world, but I immediately felt a connection with this young man, as I knew what was in store for him: the excitement and panic, the happiness and disappointment, the success and failure.

Around the same time, I heard from an old colleague,

someone who had worked for me when I ran a factory in Turkey throughout the '70s, before I fled the country in fear for my family's safety amid growing political violence. He reached out to tell me about the success he had found in the years since, eventually starting his own factories worth millions and employing hundreds of people. He also told me that he owed much of his success to my guidance when we worked together, claiming that I had not only shown him how to be a good engineer, but a good person as well.

I thought a lot about my interview with Cenk, the resulting comments, and the influence I had had on my former employee, among others whom I have met in my life, and I wondered if maybe there was some gas in my tank yet. I've worn many hats—farmer, student, immigrant, engineer, entrepreneur, son, brother, husband, father, grandfather—and in that time I've seen the world change in surprising and profound ways, some for the better and, unfortunately, some for the worse. Maybe I could use the knowledge I've gained in my many years to help others, young and old, live their best lives.

Now more than ever, guidance is needed here in the US, in a country that seems to be moving backward. America's not alone of course, as a trend toward fighting progress is occurring in many places. The US holds a special spot in my heart, though, as it offered me so many opportunities when I first came here as an immigrant. The American people treated me with kindness, respect, and love. They helped me and hoped I would succeed.

I never experienced any xenophobic attitudes or anti-immigrant sentiments. People's care and congeniality amazed me.

Contrasted to many contemporary attitudes, spurred on by the current administration, it's like night and day. I worry that many people have forgotten that the US once tried to welcome all people in all their diversity. I understand what is meant by the terms "legal" and "illegal" immigrants, documented and undocumented, but to me, these are just words. No matter where someone emigrates from, or immigrates to, we all deserve a chance to achieve success and freedom, the type that only comes through opportunities, like those I'm proud to say I received both in Turkey and in the US.

The odds aren't just stacked against immigrants today either. According to a 2017 study by Credit Suisse, most millennials are financially worse off than the generation before them at the same age, despite being more highly trained and educated. Many are facing crushing college debt in an economy and job market where inequality has grown, widening the gap between rich and poor Americans. In 2016, the Equality of Opportunity Project, now called Opportunity Insights, reported that the chances of children earning more than their parents during their lifetime was around 50 percent, whereas in 1940 it was 90 percent. This all likely contributes to the fact that, as of 2017, less than 20 percent of Americans said they were living the American Dream, as found by the Hearth Insights' 2017 State of the American Dream report.

Without hard work and determination, we rarely go far. But even pulling ourselves up by the bootstraps requires the support and kindness of others and policies that provide opportunities for all. These elements are integral to personal and professional success, not to mention the success of our country, society, and world—a world that we all hope to be proud of. We need to follow tried and true lessons that are often overlooked, such as the importance of family, hard work, and seizing opportunities, while also embracing more nuanced approaches to life, questioning our own beliefs and assumptions, taking risks we believe in—no matter what others think—and approaching our careers with an entrepreneurial mindset.

My life's story is not remarkable, and I've never exaggerated or embellished my experiences. I haven't written this book to make millions, nor simply for posterity's sake, but to help those people looking for a roadmap to success, while telling the story of a regular working man's life over the past eighty-plus years. So often, history is told from the top down, skewing toward political leaders, famous celebrities, ruling parties, and the elite. Instead, this story is my story: how a young boy from an agricultural town most people have never heard of managed to attain a sliver of the American Dream, and how anyone else, no matter where they're from or the obstacles they face, can do so as well, through persistence, gumption, and a little bit of help.

1

A Boy of Kilis

THE WAR WAS ON, BUT it was a world away. Turkey hadn't yet entered the fray, staying neutral between the Axis and the Allies until February of 1945, when the country could no longer keep its distance. The men of Kilis, a large, provincial agricultural town in the Gaziantep province of Turkey, spoke of the war often, how the Germans fought bravely but both sides were valiant in their efforts.

I'd listen to their stories out in front of my mother's house, wrapped up in tales of fierce battles and hand-to-hand combat. Most of them scared me—the sheer number of people who had died in the war up until that point was unimaginable to a boy my age—but I liked to dream of the far off places they spoke of, Germany and France, Russia and Japan, and, one of my favorites, America. As I grew up, my interest in America never waned. It grew as I grew, and I knew one day I'd find myself there, or so I hoped.

Many early mornings, right after the sun had come up and dawn had given way to day, I would lie in a wheat field waiting for a *shahraci*, a type of farmer who transported crops by donkey to a harvest area outside the center of town. Staring up at the sky, I thought about what was happening beyond the farmlands of Kilis, outside of the country, far away. I watched the clouds roll by in wonder and imagined planes above, the same flown by the Americans, the Germans, the Japanese.

My other favorite daydream was about getting out of work.

Even then, I was devising a plan, a great plan, to get an education, leave farm life behind, and meet and marry a beautiful girl—for an eight-year-old boy, it was quite ambitious and detailed.

My father had died when I was just eight months old, so though I'd love to say I knew him, that would be a lie. He was young, only thirty-seven, when he succumbed to cancer, leaving my mother, Nuriye, my six-year-old brother, Ihsan, and me to fend for ourselves. Ihsan had been old enough to remember him, but only vaguely.

With my father gone, the rest of us had to work ever harder, my mother taking on the lion's share, though both Ihsan and I pulled our weight. On account of his illness, when my dad passed away there was a sizable number of medical bills left for us to handle, adding up to tens of thousands in today's US dollars—tens of thousands we certainly didn't have. My mom borrowed some money from our uncles and other relatives, then took out a loan to start paying down the rest of this huge debt.

City of Kilis, Turkey, circa 1940.

Like many other families in Kilis, we lived simply, making money from the plots of land we cultivated and the crops we harvested. Kilis is located two miles north of the Syrian border on a long, even stretch of land. Mountains loom above to the north, but looking off to the east, west, and south, it's flat as far as the eye can see. The town had become an agricultural center on account of this terrain and its good soil. Kilis is located close to the Fertile Crescent, which stretches like a half-moon from the Persian Gulf to the Mediterranean Sea, extending from Iraq to Egypt, and covering the southland mass of Turkey. As far back as 5000–4000 BC, human societies started to settle throughout this area and develop agriculture and farming methods.

My mother owned six small plots, most of which were

entirely inconveniently located to one another. The only pieces of land that were next to each other were two tiny agricultural lots about a mile or so from our house. There we would grow and cultivate small amounts of cotton or wheat, as much as the minuscule space could bear. Another piece of land we owned was a vineyard with about 350 grape vines three miles from our home. The three other plots consisted of olive trees—one with fifteen trees, one with twelve, and one right over the border in Syria that held twenty. None of the olive groves were close to our home, near the center of Kilis, nor were they near the grape vines, nor were they near each other. This meant we had to travel miles in all sorts of different directions to check in on the crops. Though I find it funny now, it was no laughing matter for us then.

Unlike many of the other farmers, we didn't have any transportation—no donkeys, no horses, and, of course, no tractors. Though we would have been considered a middle-class family, we were low on the middle-class ladder, near the bottom rungs. Members of the "lower classes" worked in the fields as well, but they also built houses, held construction jobs, and cleaned the streets, while some were merchants who owned small grocery stores or butcher shops. None of them owned their own land. Just as today, land ownership was important, and the wealthiest families had the most land—the biggest commodity in any agricultural area. Therefore, we were fortunate to have our own pieces of land, but that didn't change the fact that they were difficult to get to.

I started to work in the fields when I was seven or eight

years old. When I was in grammar school, I would help my mom out before and after class and then throughout the entire summer. Though I began contributing to the family by performing small chores around the house, in no time I was pulling and cutting weeds, checking fruit, and tending to the crops. When we were lucky, my uncle let us use his horses and donkeys. On such occasions, I would stay overnight at his house and then get up at 3:00 a.m. The town slept as I rode down the streets through the eerie calm of those quiet, dark mornings. Whenever I heard something off in the distance, my boyhood imagination would get the best of me, uncertain of what might be lurking in the shadows. With chills running down my spine, I'd hurry the animal along.

More often than not, I had to be up around 4:00 or 4:30, then walk at least an hour before beginning my duties for the day. Tending 350 grape vines adds up to a lot of grapes, and I spent many early mornings, the light barely creeping up from the east, checking each and every vine, the sweet juice of the fruit drying on my fingers. When it came time to harvest the crops, we would hire on an additional set or two of hands and some horses or donkeys when we could afford them. Our relatives in town were also always willing to help, so between them and the people we hired, we were able to transfer our harvest.

Throughout the area, grapes were a popular commodity, and my family and the others in Kilis had all sorts of uses for them. Though we didn't make wine, there was a wine factory in town, despite Kilis being predominantly Muslim. We probably would have sold grapes to the factory too, but we typically used almost 90 percent of the food we produced and had regular buyers for the other 10 percent. We crushed the grapes and drained the juice, making a heavy grape paste sweetener, a taste I have never forgotten. Commercially, this sweetener would be mixed with water and sold at stores or markets. Many people would combine the paste with fresh-made tahini and then slather it on bread for breakfast or a midday snack.

My favorite thing my mother used the sweetener for was homemade candy. She would tie halves of hazelnuts or almonds on a piece of string, dip the string into the grape paste, let it dry for a moment, then dip it again. She'd repeat this process until the string and the nuts were entirely coated, and then hang the string to dry. Come wintertime, when we had visitors, my mother would snip off portions to share with our guests, though my brother and I also used to cut off small pieces throughout the year that we would hide in our pockets and eat on the way to school. We didn't have chocolate or any sugary sweets, but I wouldn't have traded this grape candy for all the Hershey's bars in the world.

Grape season went from July through September, but the olive-harvesting season started later in the year and lasted through November or December. With our olive groves spread out in a number of locations, on some days we'd have to retrace our steps and backtrack past certain plots just to get to others. But from those olives, we pressed the most incredible olive oil.

Of course, we couldn't just live off of olive oil and sweet grape paste, though I'm sure my mother would have liked to try. We traded with other farmers occasionally, but mostly sold any of the crops we didn't use. Some of the money we made also went toward essentials like food and clothing, but we produced much of our own. There was no need for imports and we bought very few things. We had no electricity, no refrigerator, so any food we made or prepared had to be eaten by the following morning. Just like many of the other farmers in our town, we were self-sustaining, right down to the clothing we wore, most of which was created from cotton we picked from our field.

Everything was manual then, so just like the grapes and olives, the cotton was harvested by hand. Before we could bring the cotton home or drop it off to sell at a market in town, we first had to carry it to a small processing center so the seeds could be extracted, a labor-intensive process in which the seeds had to be plucked or massaged out with sticks. From there, we would take the seedless cotton to a place in Kilis called *Halash*, which was another processing center. When we got to *Halash*, we handed the cotton over to a small group of men. They took long, curved pieces of wood that had strings attached to them, forming bows, and hit the cotton. We'd get the chance to take a break then, watching the men whack away at the crop, enlarging it as it became floppy and pliable. But we didn't have long to rest on our laurels. As soon as they finished, we brought that processed cotton to the market or to our home.

For a number of years while I was young, one of my mother's older, distant relatives lived with us, and we came to call her "grandmother." Grandmother was a sweet old woman, and we had more than enough room to share in our home—it just being my mother, Ihsan, and I—so we were all happy to have her. As part of the family, we took care of her; in return, she helped as much as she could. When we brought the cotton home, it was her time to shine. As with many houses in the area, ours had an open-air courtyard around which were doors leading to separate rooms. In the center of the courtyard, we had a well for water and an area where we grew flowers and some other plants, including a few more grape vines for good measure. Grandmother would sit in the courtyard with a small wooden machine—a primitive set up with a barrel on a few legs—and thread the cotton through the machine's needle hole, producing a yarn-like string.

Then we were off again with the string to visit a *choolha*. *Choolhas* were men in town who handled the dying and weaving of the cotton. They would take the string, place it into colored dyes, let it dry, and then, using a giant loom, weave it into pieces of fabric. We would bring this fabric to my mother, who would later cut it up and sew it into linens and clothing. I wore clothing like this—shirts, pants, and underwear—all the way up until high school; clothing we had produced with the help of the surrounding community, from the field to our backs.

For a few summers we grew wheat, which is why one of the *shahracis* would find me waiting around in the mornings, lounging in the wheat fields, when I probably should have been working. But this wheat, this goddamn wheat, was something else—worse than the grapes, the olives, and the cotton combined.

When the crop was ready to cut, our uncles, cousins, and anyone we were able to hire, would all head out into the field with us. Together, we would chop away at the base of the wheat, then place it into towering stacks. A *shahraci* would come by with donkeys, and we'd strap the wheat to the animals, then follow along as they carried it out to a harvest area, called the *harman yeri*. These were long, hot days, covered in dirt, our sweat mixing in to create a thin layer of grime across our forearms and faces.

All of the staple crops, like wheat or barley, were transported to the *harman yeri*, where they would be cut into a manageable size. To do this, we first grouped the crop—wheat in our case—into piles on the ground. We then employed a rudimentary machine that looked something like a wooden cart with two large rollers in the front and two in the back, all four of which were covered in blades. Either a horse or donkey were connected to this cart-like machine, and someone sat atop it to direct the animal to move forward in a circle. As the animal walked, the rollers went over the wheat, cutting it into smaller and smaller pieces. The crop would fly in all directions, so we'd have to stop every so often to gather it back into piles. This process was repeated until the wheat was chopped up into short, one to one-and-a-half inch pieces.

Skilled farmers would then come by to separate out the chaff by throwing these piles high up in the air, the chaff landing in one place and the useable portion of the wheat landing in another. The chaff was only used for animal feed, and since we didn't own any animals, we would sell that part right then and there, bag up our wheat, and finally go home for the night.

Grain processing fields outside of Kilis, Turkey, circa 1950.

My mother used the wheat for all sorts of purposes, making flour, starch, and bulgur. Most importantly, she baked fresh bread almost every day. Starting with the dough, she would roll it, pound it, and knead it, before placing it into beat up, old clay crocks that were two to three feet in diameter. Though these crocks were typically used to store olive oil or other liquids, ferment pickles, or save dried goods, my mother—always extremely conscious about our finances—reused these containers for cooking, attaching them to the wall and heating the dough in them over an open fire. It was a lot of work, but it paid off—the bread was delicious.

As for our food, that was basically it: olives, grapes, and wheat made up the majority of our diet. We had access to few vegetables or other fruits, though we'd sometimes receive an orange or apple on a special occasion. Mostly, if we hadn't grown it and harvested it ourselves, then we didn't have access to it.

At the end of each day we were all exhausted; my hands would be torn up and blistered, my legs sore, and I would stink to high hell. It was a hard way to make a living. If all of those plots had been in one place, or if we could have hired more help, it might have been different, but then again, our situation wasn't all that uncommon. The work was difficult. It wasn't an easy life, but it was a shared one. Not only did I have Ihsan and my mother, but also Grandmother, my uncles and aunts, my cousins, and the other members of the town. This way of life helped create a bond between the members of our family and built a tight-knit community, one to which I would find myself indebted again and again throughout the years.

And growing up, it wasn't all just hard work.

Like many young boys, one of my favorite things to do was go to the movies. There was a theater in the center of town that showed Turkish and American films, and later some from India, but the ones from the US grabbed my attention unlike any others, mostly cowboy westerns.

I'd stare at the screen transfixed, and afterward, I would act out scenes from them, attempting accents and saying American phrases I didn't understand. This early love of acting was only compounded the first time I saw a group of students from the Gaziantep high school perform a play in Kilis by the seventeenth century French playwright Molière. I went to the performance by myself, and just like at the movies, as soon as I sat in the theater, I was mesmerized. I had never seen anything like it before.

It was always a treat to go to the movies with my friends or family, but on special occasions, we would attend the cinema for, of all things, a wedding. The bride and groom would stand up and exchange vows right in front of the screen as the people they'd invited sat in the audience, which would normally be full. There were two chairs and a small table set up in the front as well, so once the ceremony concluded, the bride and groom could take their seats and, together with the audience, watch whatever movie was playing. And that was it—that was their wedding! I clearly remember attending three or four of them, including my cousin's, and they're some of my favorite weddings I've ever been to.

Not only were these celebrations special because of where they took place, but in general weddings were a particularly exciting event, since no one in town celebrated birthdays, anniversaries, or holidays of that sort. Even if we had wanted to celebrate our birthdays, it wouldn't have been possible for many of us, including me, since birth certificates were not issued at that time.

I know I was born in the year 1937, but my exact

birthday is unknown. When I asked my mother about this once, she told me that it took place around the time "when the black grapes are ripe to eat"—talk about a true agricultural society. As I got older I realized this meant I must have been born somewhere around the end of July or beginning of August, but no one knew for sure, and no one seemed to care. Each town in Turkey eventually created a town registry, so when my name was added to the one in Kilis, January 1, 1937 was listed as the day I was born, which has stuck ever since. It's understandable: they couldn't have written "grape-picking season" or "when the black grapes are ripe to eat" on the form, so I couldn't blame them.

It may sound odd now, but none of this was a big deal to my mother or the rest of our family, since so few of us knew our actual birthdates. Some of the wealthier families kept track of these dates by writing them down on the opening blank page inside of their family Quran. Though every household had one, few of the families we knew used them as the family ledger. In the end, we didn't care one way or another, it was just normal for us.

We had a big extended family, both on my mother's and father's sides, and when not working the lands, we spent much of our time together. After my dad passed away, my mother's sister and her family visited often, as did my father's brother, my uncle Huseyin Aga. Huseyin Aga used to come to our house almost every day to talk to my mother and check in on us. "Aga" was a term used to signify land ownership and importance within the community, and Huseyin Aga owned a couple of properties in Kilis, including an extensive vineyard. He was well respected throughout town.

Despite never having known my father, I never felt lonely, as I found father figures in my uncles and other members of the community. Both Huseyin Aga and his eldest son, Ismail Agabey, treated me like a son. Ismail Agabey had three sons very close to my age, and we played together almost every day, as if I was the fourth brother. My family was warm, friendly, and welcoming, and I grew up loved. That taught me my earliest values— the basics of being good to other people.

All my family lived within walking distance, so we would get together to play in the streets or fields, swap stories, and eat meals together. Though the war had been the main topic among the men then, they talked of local news as well and what was going on in Gaziantep, which was about an hour-and-a-half drive from the center of Kilis. There wasn't a standard daily, weekly, or monthly meeting, nothing like that; all of these discussions were casual and continuous, everyone passing news or gossip back and forth. When I was that age, Kilis didn't have a local newspaper, and it wouldn't for another five or ten years—even then, it was limited. There were newspapers printed in Ankara, Turkey's capital, and Istanbul, but as a boy I wasn't encouraged to read them, or anything else for that matter. There was one small library in town and one at the school, neither of which had many books. No one really taught us that reading was important.

This casual sharing of information and lack of outside

influence contributed to the insularity of the community, and a limited exposure to the world beyond the fields of my hometown. We all knew each other and supported each other in a way that can only come from living in a small community of that kind. Always having people to talk to, or other children to play with, those early years in Kilis are baked into my memories as joyous ones, even though I was already planning my escape.

Another reason people gathered at my mother's house so often was because she was something of an unofficial judge in the neighborhood, both among my extended family and other community members. She didn't have much formal education, aside from religious school, where she learned to read Arabic. She actually couldn't write in Turkish. Many years earlier, her brothers refused to let her learn, chiding her teachers not to teach her, in fear that she would write lover letters to boyfriends—boyfriends she didn't have in reality. It's strange to think what else she could have accomplished if she had been raised in a more progressive environment, and as I got older I felt bad for her, feeling some of her potential had been squandered. If she ever felt that way, though, she never let on.

Despite a lack of formal schooling, she was incredibly smart and logical. I believe one of the reasons people came to her so often was because she was wise and knowledgeable in a way that can't easily come from school alone. My mother was recognized throughout the community as someone who could help solve problems, mostly mediating what I would call "family disputes."

Most families in Kilis lived with their extended family, including their in-laws, which led to more bickering, tiffs, and quarrels than anything else, especially between mothers-in-law and their daughters-in-law.

Though that sounds stereotypical, it played out to be true time and time again. Often, the daughters-in-law would approach my mother, explaining the situation. A common complaint was that they felt they couldn't meet their mothers-in-law's unreasonably high standards. Arranged marriages were traditional and widespread when I was growing up, and the mothers were always trying to make sure the wives chosen for their sons were the smartest, most skilled, most attractive, and so on—it's no surprise that these brides didn't always live up to the unrealistic expectations placed upon them. So they came to my mother to talk, hoping to sort out some of these ongoing spats. Similarly, husbands and wives met with her regularly to discuss issues they were going through and to ask her advice. In this way, she was almost like a psychiatrist as well.

Many families also came to speak with her about inheritance problems. For example, if somebody died with a few pieces of real estate to their name, but it was unclear who they should have been left to within the family, this could lead to major headaches, or much worse. With the importance of land being paramount, essential to our existence, it's understandable that disputes were likely to arise when land was on the line. But people listened to her. She walked them through the steps, told them to be reasonable, and they always respected her

THE ORIGINAL YOUNG TURK | 17

suggestions and advice on how to move forward without creating further issues.

These types of problems were bound to come up in a small town, and since there wasn't a set system for how to deal with them, my mother was the de facto word of law, an informal Judge Judy of the day. There weren't many women like her in town either; she was unique. She spoke her mind and was open with her opinions. People were always surprised to see her stop in the middle of the main road in town to chat with the government officials who came through Kilis to check on the state of things. They'd talk for a half hour or so, which was uncommon, and ask her all sorts of questions, taking her responses seriously. They understood she was a respected woman in town, with her finger on the pulse of Kilis. As time passed, people only admired her more for her strength, wisdom, and reputation.

It also didn't hurt her standing that our family held deep roots in Kilis, starting with my great, great grandfather—Molla Habip—who arrived there in 1839. In his early twenties, Habip had enlisted in the Ottoman Empire army, which had been making its way toward southern Turkey when it stopped in Karaman, the town where Habip had lived all his life. Turmoil had erupted between the Ottoman Empire and Egypt, as they had rebelled against the Ottoman state. The Egyptian military began occupying land from Egypt up through parts of Syria and southern Turkey, including Kilis. The sultan of the Ottoman Empire, Mahmud II, sent his general, what was called a *Pasha* in Turkish, to put down this uprising, and as he travelled from Istanbul down south, he recruited many young troops, including Habip.

The Pasha led his troops to a town called Nizip, about seventy-five miles northeast of Kilis, where they engaged the Egyptian army. The Ottoman army proved to be unprepared, or had underestimated the strength of the uprising, and their troops were squashed by Egypt's. The headquarters of the Egyptian army was based in Kilis, and the Egyptian commander brought many of the Ottoman troops back to town. After concessions were made, he released many of them, Habip being one. Karaman was about 350 miles away, no small journey in 1839, so he decided to stay put. He settled in the growing agricultural village and started a family.

As his family grew, so did Kilis. When I was born, the village had sprouted into a town of 25,000 people and both my mother's and father's families had become well established.

It's also possible that people looked to my mother for guidance because of her religious background, though this in itself was a complex situation. My mother was highly religious, having even performed the Hajj, the annual Islamic pilgrimage to Mecca—the holiest city for Muslims—that every Muslim is theoretically supposed to partake in during their lifetimes. She also used to pray five times a day and read the Quran at least three times a year. Many people, especially members of her generation and older, respected her religiosity and the worldview brought about by her faith. The younger people in town, such as the daughters-in-law who would often visit her, saw that she had lived through an evolving Turkey. They took this life experience into account when seeking her advice, helping them put her religious beliefs in context, since Islam's influence in Turkey had significantly changed during her life, affecting the culture profoundly.

When I was a child, Turkey had recently gone through a major shift in both its politics and religion, brought on by the diminished power of the Ottoman Empire, which, by 1918, had been relegated to Istanbul alone, and was dissolved entirely on November 1, 1922. This was a massive restructuring of political order, as the Ottoman Empire had been established over six-hundred years earlier, in 1300, at Northwest Anatolia. By 1453, the Ottomans had captured Istanbul and marched into the European heartland, reaching their zenith in 1560 with Solomon the Magnificent.

Unfortunately, the Ottomans refused to recognize the European Renaissance, the Age of Enlightenment, any type of religious reformation, and, most importantly, the powers of overseas trade and treaties. The Ottoman state didn't wake up until a period from 1740 to 1850, but they were too late—by then, they were unable to reform the whole state's structure in time to catch up with Europe's.

World War I was the empire's death rattle, while in its wake the Turkish War of Independence led to the establishment of a new Turkish state, the Republic of Turkey, on October 29, 1923, by Mustafa Kemal Ataturk. The Ottoman Empire had been an Islamic one, but by the turn of the twentieth-century, many people in Turkey had lost their faith and pride in the Ottomans and the new state was welcomed with open arms, along with Ataturk's reforms on religion, law, politics, and culture.

As a boy, we were still living under Ataturk's revolution, one that supported secularity over religion and believed in the separation of church and state. Ataturk had disbanded the caliphate, which had been connected to the Ottoman Empire, meaning the country was no longer under the authority of an Islamic "caliph," or leader. With the end of this Islamic rule, most people who grew up in that atmosphere became fiercely independent seculars.

When Ataturk established the Republic, he created a new school system as well, void of religious influence. Therefore, throughout primary school, and well on through middle school and high school, my teachers were all progressive, educating us with the type of fact-based information, science, history, art, and developed-world curriculum that hadn't been given attention during the Ottoman reign. So they didn't teach us anything religious at all, creating somewhat of a small rift between generations.

My mother tried sending me to a religious school one summer when I was still young. My cousin Alaeddin and I went together, sat in class, and attempted to follow along. Being rambunctious kids, we weren't much for school then, so as we listened to the teacher discuss the importance of the Quran, explaining how it was a book sent from the sky by Allah, we both found ourselves distracted and began talking to one another. I had only said a few words when the teacher came storming back from the front of the class with a long stick in his hand.

Before I had the chance to apologize or explain myself, he smacked me on the top of my head.

That was is it for my formal religious education—we left that day and we didn't go back. (Not long ago, while in Turkey, I saw Alaeddin and we laughed about this story, as he remembers that day well.) I thought my mom would be furious when I told her I wouldn't be going anymore, but she simply said, "Fine, if you don't want to go, don't go," and put me to work once again the next morning. If I had thought it through more, it may have been a good way to stay out of the fields, but for once I was happy to return to my chores.

Neither my brother nor I, nor any of the other young people in our families, prayed or went to mosque, except for on special occasions or holidays, such as the first day after Ramadan. We still considered ourselves Muslims and some of the traditions stuck—I actually fasted one month a year during Ramadan until I was forty-five years old—but religion wasn't central to our lives. Not to say it wasn't important to some members of the community. There were plenty of people who strictly followed Islam and its tenants, praying five times daily, attending mosque regularly, and sending their children to solely religious schools. But there was no pressure from society, family, or anyone else to be observant, and it didn't affect our friendships or relationships in the community. Many of my friends in the neighborhood held onto their families' old religious beliefs, and though that created a natural divide, none of us took issue with our differences.

It wasn't just religion that Ataturk focused on either, he had set his sights on a full top-to-bottom modernization, a contemporary Turkey that could one day compete with other major world powers. For example, women achieved the right to vote in 1930. He also switched the official alphabet of Turkey from Arabic characters to Roman letters and ensured that all Turkish citizens standardized an official surname for their families, which was not previously the practice. So in 1927, just ten years before I was born, my family settled on the last name "Uygur," which had come at the suggestion of one of our relatives who worked for the education ministry in Ankara.

Though our relatives locally shared a family name, Molla Habip Oglu, it was long and difficult to pronounce, and it wasn't used by all the members of our family throughout Turkey anyhow. As our relative in Ankara explained, the "Uygurs" had been the most educated Turks in all of central Asia and had run China. They managed the affairs and political states of Turkish tribes in the country, Central Asia, and parts of the Middle East. Apparently all of Genghis Khan's bureaucrats, or government officials, were Uygurs. Even though most of my family, like my mom, didn't put a high value on formal education, they liked the name, as it symbolized intelligence and importance.

On a larger level, Ataturk presented Turkey, and what it meant to be Turkish, in an entirely new way. He was famous for his phrase "Yurtta sulh, cihanda sulh," meaning "Peace at home, peace in the world." When he was asked what he wanted his legacy to be, he explained that when he was gone, he didn't want to leave any rules or regulations behind that couldn't be changed or altered, that couldn't modernize. He understood that the world was always evolving and he wanted the Turkish people to evolve with it, following science and truth, nothing else.

I can't emphasize enough how monumental Ataturk's influence was on Turkey during and after World War I, and how much that affected my life in Kilis. If there had been no Ataturk, if the Ottoman Empire had somehow continued, I would be a 100 percent different person than I am today.

Without my family and the Kilis community, however, I would be nothing.

Though I didn't realize it then, my young days in Kilis were foundational in a way that would reverberate throughout my life. The support of my family, and the support provided to my family by the surrounding community, gave me a chance that many will never be fortunate enough to receive. With my father gone, my family banded together even closer, my uncles and older cousins, and my brother later on, acting as father figures. My mother's strength was incredible, and I still think of her in awe, her ability to raise us right, her willingness to endure backbreaking work for our sake day in and day out. And just as everyone in the extended family and in our community helped her, she helped them.

Though insularity holds its own set of problems, it can also create a unique type of interdependence. In Kilis, we had no one else except each other, so we took care of each other whole-heartedly, looked after our own, and worked with one another to not only survive, but thrive together. I know not everyone is that lucky, and not all communities are the same, but there's always a way to become part of a community, and that's by surrounding one's self with positive influences and good people. Though the world is abuzz with digital and online communities today, which have merits as well, there's nothing like in-person, face-to-face interaction to build social capital and help lead a fulfilling life, whether at work, recreationally, or at home.

I knew I would leave Kilis some day—after all, that was my boyhood plan—but it wasn't truly just to get out of work and off the farm. I wanted to make something of myself, and even at that age, I knew that I wanted to do something to give back to my family—my mother, my brother, my uncles and aunts and cousins, my community—to show them the support they had shown me. As I got older, I was able to do just that.

One evening, after I had come home from the vineyard, my family and I ate supper together. It was a quiet night, and I decided to walk out onto the balcony that was off to the side of our house, a place we often slept during the summer months to stay cool after the sweltering days. I also liked visiting the balcony alone for the chance to hear myself think.

The stars were just coming out, the moon resting among them, and I lay down to daydream once again, thinking about my life and what may come. I looked up at the sky, wondering what might be out there, and I imagined my future, so uncertain at such a young age.

I felt at that moment that anything was possible. I didn't know what was ahead of me, but even then I had the sense it was something more than my immediate surroundings. The strength and care of my family and the community would sustain me and guide me throughout my life, but right then, I was ready for something new, something grand.

First, however, I had to get started on my plan.

2

School Days

THOUGH MY PLAN RELIED ON receiving a strong education, I wasn't the best student. In fact, I wasn't a very good student at all. I had been held back in first grade and had to repeat the year all over again, setting a tone for grade school that was not easily shaken off.

With my mother's lack of schooling, she never put a high value on book smarts. She certainly wasn't pleased with me having to repeat the first grade, but it was more important to her that I helped with the farming and chores than receive straight As—not that I was receiving any As anyhow. I just didn't have someone to set me on the right path and encourage my education.

I don't blame my family; they had so many other concerns to simply make a living from day to day. If education didn't fit into their lives, and wasn't going to help them in planting, picking, and harvesting their crops, then they didn't see much use in it.

My brother broke away from this mold. Five years older than me, Ihsan had quietly been making plans of his own, and he wasn't distracted by my actions or behavior. After failing first grade, I tried a bit harder, though I was anything but a stellar student. Ihsan had always looked out for me when we were kids, though he never seemed worried about my childhood shortcomings, whether at school or when whiling away when I should have been helping in the fields. When I started getting a little older, I think he began noticing I was getting off track and felt that I needed direction.

We mostly got along, but as brothers manage to do, we got in fights with one another from time to time. One early morning when I was twelve, I tried sneaking out of the house to avoid my daily chores, hoping that I could slip away and off to a park in town to hide out undetected. I had done so repeatedly, and both my mother and brother were getting fed up with me shirking my responsibilities, especially now that I was hitting adolescence.

As I tiptoed out the front door, I felt Ihsan's strong grip on my shoulders, the hands of a young man who'd worked the fields his whole life. He turned me around and leaned forward, bending down slightly to stare me sternly in the eye. "Come inside," he said, "we need to talk."

I was scared that he'd yell at me, or worse, but I followed him into the house anyhow. He called me into the kitchen where he was standing at the table.

"Sit down," he said.

I hesitantly pulled out a chair next to him and followed his command.

"Look," he continued, "here's the deal. I know you don't want to stick around here your whole life—neither do I. But right now, we don't have any other way to make money. Without Dad, and with Mom so busy, we need to rely on each other and work together, at home or out in the vineyard and olive groves or even in school. If you study your ass off and get your shit together, you can do anything you want—become a doctor or a lawyer, a businessman, anything—and one day, when you're a father, you can make a better life for you and your family."

His speech seemed rehearsed, as if he'd been waiting for the perfect time to recite it to me. I couldn't find the words to respond—I was floored—so I just nodded in assent and thanked him. Then we got our gear together and walked out to the vineyard.

We worked alongside each other all day, and Ihsan made a few jokes to lighten the mood, but, over and over again, I kept thinking of what he had said in the kitchen. Though I'd always wanted to get an education and leave Kilis, I had never really thought about what it would be like to have a family of my own, one to care for and support, like mine did for me.

Though my uncles and eldest cousins had acted as father figures up until then, starting that morning, my brother assumed this role, beginning a lifetime of inspiration that I am forever grateful for. When I went to bed that night, tired and sore as usual, I couldn't sleep due to the thoughts rattling around in my head. I finally dozed off, but awoke in a cold sweat in the middle of the night, worried about my future, a mini pre-teen existential crisis.

The next day, I got up and looked over a recent report card of mine, noting the dismal grades. I made a promise then and there to start fresh: from then on, education would become the center of my life. I watched with pride as my brother finished high school and went to college that fall, the first one to do so in our family, both on my mother's and father's sides. While many people his age were content to stay in Kilis and carry on their families' farms and lifestyles, Ihsan had applied himself and passed the university entrance exams.

Ever since Ataturk established the new Turkish state, public education was free for everyone up through high school, and college was free for those students who passed the university entrance exams. Without such an opportunity, my mother would have never been able to send Ihsan to college. So though she was stuck paying off our family's debts, Ihsan was able to afford school, and he set off for Ankara to continue his education.

Inspired by Ihsan, I further immersed myself in my studies, making sure I too would someday go to college. Any free time I had, I put toward learning, even after long days in the fields. I started to try—to really try—and it turned out that some of the subjects I had feared most weren't so bad after all.

Take mathematics: I previously had no interest in the topic. It seemed too difficult and, frankly, boring, so I mostly wondered, "What's the use?" When I started to actually concentrate on the work, it wasn't nearly as complicated as I had once thought. And, to my surprise, I enjoyed it. After getting down the basics—and paying attention in class—I was on a roll. I did my homework and watched my test scores soar.

My teacher was surprised with my improved performance, so much so that he assumed it was too good to be true. After class one day, he asked me to wait while the other students filed out. Once they all left, he looked me straight in the eyes and said, "Now come on, what's going on here?"

"What do you mean?" I asked.

"There's no way you're doing this all on your own. You're copying from one of your friends, right?"

Though I could have been offended, I didn't really have the right to be. I wasn't cheating, but I understood why he would be suspicious. Instead, I told him I could discuss the subjects we'd currently been studying or retake the most recent tests if he needed me to. Satisfied with my response, he told me to keep it up, but even after that, I always noticed him keeping an extra close eye on me when taking tests in class. It didn't bother me, though, as I knew I'd be out of there soon.

There was no high school in Kilis, so when I turned fourteen, I started to prepare myself to move to Gaziantep the following year. It was an odd sensation, knowing that I'd be away from home in a much larger place that I knew little about. My mother had already found a room for rent for me not far from where I'd be going to school. It wasn't uncommon then for a fourteen- or fifteen-year-old boy to live in an apartment or boarding house without his family—that was just life sometimes. I was nervous, but more than anything I was excited for the change, and the fall of 1953 couldn't come soon enough. When you're that age, however, a year can seem like a lifetime.

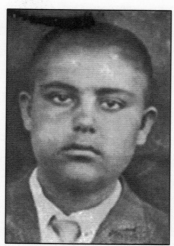

15 year old, Dogan Uygur, 1952.

The days dragged on between my middle school classes and working with my mother and a few farmhands she was able to hire earlier that year. One morning in November, she and I hiked out to our olive grove that sat just beyond the border of Turkey, in Syria, to check in on the progress of the olives and pick those that were ripe. My Uncle Mahmut always joined us on these excursions, as he had a grove of twenty olive trees right next to ours. He had made a deal with nearby villagers to tend to both groves, so we only had to go there when it was time to harvest the fruit. Though crossing the border between Turkey and Syria was somewhat casual, we had to fill out forms and receive written permission at the beginning of each year. We'd never had a problem, passing freely between the countries without issue.

When we arrived that day, we got to work as usual, inspecting and picking the olives. I was looking forward to a long break from this type of work while I attended high school in Gaziantep. In a way though, it made me enjoy those daily routines, knowing that I'd be free from them soon, if only temporarily—all the way up through college, whenever I was home, I'd help my mother with her patches of land. I was smiling, thinking about my escape, when I heard someone shouting from behind us. I turned to look and saw two men approaching, both who appeared to be Syrian soldiers.

All three of us stopped working, and my uncle walked up to them, ready to show the forms that gave us permission to be there. Neither of the men spoke Turkish, but they both shook their heads; they didn't need to see the papers.

For a moment, it occurred to me that they might have thought we were smugglers. Next to farming, smuggling was one of the other main industries in Kilis. My immediate family never got involved, but I'd say 25 to 30 percent of the families we knew—some friends, neighbors, and distant relatives even—smuggled goods across the border for extra money and to supplement their farming subsistence lifestyle. It wouldn't be far fetched for these soldiers to think we were part of that racket.

The men looked over at me, and I felt a lump in my throat, realizing something was wrong. Then one turned to my uncle and said, "Lira."

Mahmut shrugged in confusion and held up his open palms. At this point, my mother approached the soldiers as well, trying to figure out what the fuss was about.

"Lira, lira," the soldier said again, making a motion with his hands, as if to say, "give it over."

"What?" my uncle asked, still speaking in Turkish. "We don't have any money. There's nothing around here to buy or sell. Why would we be carrying money?"

I'm not sure if they understood what he said, but they both looked increasingly angry. I then stepped forward to hopefully make some sense of the situation, but as soon as I opened my mouth, one of the soldiers grabbed me by the throat and started yelling in Arabic. His hands were tight around my neck as I gasped for air, my mom and uncle screaming at them in Turkish, everyone shouting at once in chaotic disarray.

I started feeling lightheaded and woozy, grabbing on to the soldier's muscled forearms, trying to force him off of me. I was certain I'd pass out—maybe die. And as soon as I was convinced I was taking one of my final breaths, he let me go. Now both soldiers were pushing me, yelling as they prodded me out of the grove and onto the dirt road toward the village where they were headquartered. When I looked back, I could see my mother crying, begging them to let me go, not to hurt me. My uncle hugged her, trying to calm her worst fears.

When we got to the village, they tied me up and threw me into a stall in a tiny barn where they kept an old, dirt-caked horse. I lay there for what must have been two or three hours, in a mix of hay, manure, urine, and dirt, the acrid smells filling my nostrils, flies buzzing across my face and in my ears. There were occasional bursts of neighing from the horse while it moved around unsteadily, nearly stepping on me. Though it was the fall, it was hot inside that stall, and I began sweating from both heat and dread. I didn't know what the soldiers were going do to me next.

When they pulled me out, they sat me on the ground and removed my shoes. By then, I was covered in filth and my mouth was parched. I looked around frantically for my uncle and mother. I asked where they were, making motions with my tied hands, hoping the soldiers would understand what I meant. They didn't respond. Instead, one of them produced a long wooden reed and began whacking away at me with it, directly hitting the bottom of my feet.

Each time he landed a blow, it stung horribly, leaving thick welts along my arches and toes, the skin cracking open and beginning to bleed. I kept trying to stand up and run away, only to trip over myself or be forced down into the dirt again. Thankfully, the beating didn't last long—through teary eyes, I saw my Uncle Mahmut and my mother round the corner, along with a couple of men I didn't recognize. The soldiers stopped and stood above me, waiting.

Mahmut walked up to them and handed them two bags. The soldiers sat the bags in the dirt next to me and began pulling out containers of sugar and some other foodstuffs—salt, flour—which Mahmut later told me he had gotten in the village. They looked down at their bounty, then up, and my uncle and mother and smirked. After wrapping up the ransom, they untied my hands and feet, stood me up, and shoved me in my mother's direction.

I ran to her, dazed and frightened, but relieved that she was there, as only an hour earlier, I wasn't sure if I would ever see her again. She asked me if I was all right, and then my uncle said everything would be okay. He put his arm around my shoulders, walking me away from the soldiers, away from the village, and away from one of the worst experiences of my life.

All the way home, and for many years after, I was unable to get my mind around what had just happened. I couldn't believe how corrupt those soldiers were to rip off a bunch of farmers for nothing more than a few dried goods. I was resentful and angry, confused at how members of the military—part of the government and authorities of the state—could get away with this petty extortion.

And yet, I felt bad for the people of Syria, whose lives appeared even harder than ours. Those soldiers, throwing somebody my age into a makeshift prison just for some sugar . . . I almost pitied them. I knew where their lives were going, nowhere far, while I'd be off to Gaziantep soon.

The whole experience affected me profoundly, and I think of it often. It made me realize that if I stayed in Kilis, if I continued to live that life, these types of encounters could easily happen again. Who knew what kind of unpleasant, dangerous situations I'd be stuck negotiating? It was possible that my life might be cut short over some inconsequential matter. After that day, I became more anxious to leave, and finally, in September of the following year, I got on a bus and traveled to Gaziantep.

Though Kilis was considered a larger town in those days, it was nothing like Gaziantep, with around 400,000 people. I had been there before, but never alone. Everything felt *big*—the buildings, cars, shops, restaurants, and, most importantly, the possibilities. I didn't go out often, I didn't have any money to spend, but that was fine. My days were spent learning, and my evenings spent studying and doing homework, which is why I was there of course, though it could get lonely.

While adjusting to city life, I also felt guilty about having left my mother alone in Kilis. I knew she had friends and family to help her, but it just didn't seem right that neither Ihsan nor I were at home. I would be gone for months-long stretches, and since she didn't have a phone, I couldn't call her. But many people travelled between Kilis and Gaziantep, so I regularly heard from friends of the family and some uncles and cousins, all who kept me in the loop about goings on around Kilis and how my mother was managing without my brother and me.

She had to keep the hired help from the summer on full time to make up for my and my brother's absence. She didn't fully understand why Ihsan and I had begun pursuing our education with such vigor, but she accepted our decisions. Despite the miles between us, she also continued to try to take care of me.

Almost every week, she would go to the bus stop in Kilis and give one of the bus drivers—she knew all of them—a few stackable containers full of food that she had cooked and prepared for me. The bus driver would then stop at the entrance of Gaziantep, where my school was located, and drop the food off at the high school reception desk. So about once a week, I'd go by reception and pick up the food, a sweet reminder of home, not to mention the only chance I'd get to have a good meal. Aside from that I'd buy some bread from the bakery and a small portion of cheese, which made up most of my diet. If it weren't for my mother's home cooking, I may have starved.

Though school kept me busy, I still managed to get myself into a heap of trouble with my landlady, who caught me kissing her daughter. It was all very innocent, my first kiss, but that didn't stop her from throwing me out. Luckily by then I had made a few friends, and one let me stay with him for the remainder of the year. The following year I rented my own place in another family's house until I was able to move into the school's dormitories.

Dorm life suited me well, and I lived there throughout the rest of high school. Not only did I make new friends from all over the towns surrounding Gaziantep, but many of my buddies from Kilis also ended up living there. Almost 90 percent of us were from low- and middle-income families—we didn't have much, but we had a great time. All of us were diligent at school, appreciative of the chances we'd been given and the opportunities we had received, though we also goofed around like typical teenagers—what else was to be expected?

Just as when I was a young boy, I still loved imitating actors, and my friends would beg me to perform scenes from popular Turkish movies. Ever since seeing those high schoolers put on the Molière play in Kilis, my love of theater and movies had steadily increased. In middle school, I tried out for a small role in a school play and landed the part. Everyone in my family who came to the production told me I was fabulous, which, for a fourteen-year-old boy, was a nice ego boost. I know they were probably just being polite; still, I couldn't help but feel enthralled.

In high school, I not only put on performances for my friends, but I also acted in plays produced by the school. Though there were no dedicated theater classes, one of our teachers had been in a number of plays in Istanbul before coming to Gaziantep. He suggested to the school's administration that the students could benefit from a small theater program. They agreed, so he began casting his first production.

It was a comedic play, based off a book by a Turkish author, about a man from eastern Turkey who moves to the US at the turn of the twentieth century. After settling in Boston to work in a leather factory, he meets and marries an American woman and together they have a daughter, but he passes away when she's just a teenager. The mother finds out that her husband had owned some property in Turkey, so she and her daughter decide to move to her husband's hometown, and a fish out of the water story ensues, full of cultural and social misunderstandings, but resulting in a happy ending.

I spoke with the teacher, explaining my interest, and

he was convinced I would be good for the part of the police commissioner, a character who comes into play when the mother and daughter move to Turkey, so I accepted. From that teacher, I learned that in order to be a good actor, it was necessary to truly inhabit a role, thinking critically about the character I was playing. I asked myself what kind of person the commissioner was, his education and family, his thought processes, everything that came together to create him. Going forward I did this exercise with every role I had, connecting with my character to develop the right type of emotions or style, whether funny or sad, absurd or dramatic, romantic or devious.

Most of our schooling revolved around the more "practical" subjects—science, math, and history—so taking up acting was totally different than my day-to-day education. At that point, I was learning more than I ever had in my entire life, not just what they taught us in school, but about myself as well. For example, as an offshoot of acting, I realized how much I enjoyed reading and writing poetry. In Kilis, I had gotten a taste for poetry from one of my literature teachers in middle school, Mr. Kazim, who was an incredible performer of the pieces he read to us, but it wasn't until high school that my interest fully developed.

I had the leading role in a play my senior year, which was performed in one of the largest movie theaters in Gaziantep to a full house. That pretty much settled it: I decided I'd become an actor and work my way up to movie stardom. The idea worked with my plan to get out of Kilis and get an education; only now, I felt that I had a more solid direction, a specific goal in mind. Senior year, however, would be the last time I'd take center stage.

Throughout high school, I'd been sending letters back and forth with my brother. I would tell him about Gaziantep, my classes, and my new friends, and he would fill me in on his life in Ankara, where he had begun attending medical school. In one such letter, he described a new plan that he'd been hatching—once he received his degree, he wanted to move to America. There was apparently a shortage of doctors in the US, so new graduates from other countries were being encouraged to apply to programs in the states, get certified, and begin practicing medicine there. They had to receive additional training in America while working, but they were also given room and board and paid $150 per month—big money then, especially to a couple of kids from Kilis. I was so excited for him, and I wrote telling him my good news, that I too had a new plan: I was going to go to college, enroll in a theater program, and become an actor . . . he didn't reply.

The next time I saw Ihsan, he sat me down, not unlike how he had sat me down years before in our mother's kitchen, and told me not to do it. He said there were thousands of people trying to become actors and only very few were able to make a living. I had understood this to a certain extent, but hadn't truly thought much about it in any serious way. There was of course no guarantee that I would be one of those lucky people, no matter my amount of talent, inherent or otherwise. Ihsan said to me, "If you don't make it, you will have a miserable life—the exact opposite of what I want for you."

I'd never seen my brother so sincere, a pleading look in his eyes that told me this was important to him. He didn't just want to see me succeed, he needed to see me succeed, and he had never led me astray. Begrudgingly, I told him I understood, and though my heart was heavy, as I felt I was giving something up, he had convinced me. Instead of preparing for acting school, I started getting my applications together for a technical college, where I planned to study mechanical engineering.

This was a hard lesson to learn, but I recognized that I had made the right decision. I knew deep down that I would never be successful as an actor on the level I had imagined or hoped for. That's not to say young people pursuing an art should be discouraged to follow their dreams, but it's good to think about what they might be giving up in the process, which for me would have likely included a family, financial stability, and the chance to leave Turkey—three things that had become increasingly important to me. Everyone who is fortunate enough to have options throughout life must weigh them and consider them carefully. Mistakes are inevitable, but with a backup plan and a solid educational foundation most all mistakes are surmountable. In the end, I did what I had to for the life I wanted, and I am forever thankful to Ihsan for stepping in with his advice.

I applied to the Technical University of Istanbul, a premier educational institution in Turkey that only accepted 500 students each year from an applicant pool of around 3,500. Everyone had to take an entrance exam, which I studied for like a madman, and I was lucky to count myself among those 500 students. Many others from my high school entered colleges in the area, while others returned home to their farming communities. I, instead, was on my way to Istanbul in the fall of 1956.

Though everything had felt big in Gaziantep, everything in Istanbul felt huge, gigantic, mammoth. I was amazed by the size of the train station, the amount of people bustling every which way, on and off trains bound for all different directions to only god knows where. Istanbul is also the only city that is spread across two continents—the Asian side (Anadolu Yakasi) and the European side (Avrupa Yakasi)—which I had heard about but could scarcely believe until I was there, looking from Asia to Europe, about to board the ferry to cross the Bosphorous Strait. What a view.

My Aunt Hatice met me at the station. I'd be staying with her, along with my cousin Refik, his wife, Nigar, and their two kids, who all lived together. Hatice and I got on the ferry, and she laughed about how cautious I was, careful with each step, this being the first time I had ever been on any type of boat. I smelled the salt water of the Bosphorous and felt the fresh air whipping across the strait, tickling my face. I thought of a famous poem by Turkish poet Yahya Kemal Beyatli, in which he writes about the Bosphorous and the beauty of the surrounding landscape leading out to sea. Like much of his work, it's a lyrical poem influenced by Ottoman literature, one that strongly affected me when I was young, and continues to do so today. As I crossed that narrow waterway, it felt like the beginning of a new life, my own life.

Even though school was free to those who were accepted, I had been unable to get into a dorm my first year there, and I couldn't afford an apartment in Istanbul. So as I had done when I was young, and would continue to do so as I got older, I sought help from my family—without them, I wouldn't have made it that far, nor would I have gotten any farther. I was happy staying with Hatice, Nigar, and Refik, whose father, like mine, had passed away when he was young. It wasn't the first time Refik had helped my family out either. When my brother was accepted to his medical program in DC, Refik had paid for the flight to the US, which my mother couldn't afford.

Refik and his family were generous, kind, and caring, and I am so grateful to them for taking me in like they did. I knew it wasn't necessarily easy on any of them, but they made room for me—an eighteen-year-old, fresh out of high school—in their already overcrowded apartment. They even cooked and cleaned for me, treating me as another member of the immediate family. I helped with chores around the house whenever possible—much easier than my chores had been in Kilis—and tried to contribute in any way I could.

They were especially helpful in making me feel comfortable in Istanbul, an intimidating place for any young man. With Hatice acting like a mother and Refik playing the role of my brother, everything just seemed more manageable. I had taken to engineering, my knack for math playing a major role in my success at school, but I had the chance to enjoy my new surroundings as well. Refik and I had a great time together, often joking around like a couple of kids.

On special occasions, we'd have what were called "drinking dinners," in which the whole family would partake. These dinners were a kind of mini-celebration held by more liberal thinking Turkish families during holidays, birthdays, or if someone was visiting from out of town. The meal would last much longer than usual, and though we were all Muslim, we weren't strict Muslims, so we'd drink *raki*, an alcoholic beverage, while eating. This type of drinking culture is very different than in the US. As compared to guzzling down drinks, we drank slowly throughout the meal, getting deep into conversation. Throughout the night, everyone would become livelier, and we'd move on to telling jokes or singing Turkish folk songs.

By then, I had memorized many poems, which I loved to recite. I also used to kid around about the people from my hometown—I promise it was harmless fun—imitating their accent, which was unique compared to the one people had in Istanbul. Funny enough, whenever I saw Refik later in life, he would always bring up how I had put on these performances, and how much he had enjoyed them.

In addition to having fallen in love with poetry, my interest in western literature began growing while in Istanbul as well. When I arrived in the city, one of my distant relatives was already enrolled in the Technical

University of Istanbul, two years ahead of me. One day he took me to his home and gave me a bulky bag full of books—I was baffled. It contained all sorts of classics from Russia, England, and France, including Montaigne's *Essays*, Voltaire's *Candide*, Victor Hugo's *Les Miserables*, Honore de Balzac's *Father Goriot*, and Charles Dickens's *David Copperfield*. I had never realized how much literature could affect me. I shared them with Refik and we'd dissect them together, talking about the plots, themes, and style; how they made us feel; and what they made us think about. In reading those books, we grew together.

Even after I received government aid to enter a dorm, I would visit with Refik and his family every weekend. We had become so close, and I can never fully explain my feelings of gratitude for their help.

Despite being in such a large city, I stayed focused on the work at hand. Just as when I was in Gaziantep, I began meeting new people, but instead of them only being from the Gaziantep province, they were from all over Turkey. Most of them had come from small towns like mine, from low- and middle-income backgrounds, and had studied hard to get into school and take advantage of the free education available.

Many would later start businesses of their own, including some close friends I stayed in touch with. I found it inspiring to be surrounded by so many people working hard, taking that extra step to make a better life for themselves. And though engineering remained at the center of our educational pursuits, we were all learning about other things together as well.

In the late1950s Mediterranean culture in Istanbul, there was a type of "pickup ritual" that young men and women followed. It of course feels outdated today, maybe inappropriate, but it was the standard.

My friends and I would go out in the city, posting up somewhere along the street. If one of us saw a young woman who we thought was attractive, we'd approach her by our self and try to open a conversation with something like, "Can we be friends?" It sounds ridiculous in retrospect, especially since nine times out of ten the response we'd receive would be, "Get away from me, stupid" or something much more colorful. But that was our cue to lightly insist, once or twice, hoping that the girl wouldn't continue walking on, which she often did.

If they thought we were cute, or at least endearing, after they'd insulted us, they'd say, "What do you want?" which meant the door was now open to start a conversation with them. They had to say "no" at first, because it would have been outrageous in our culture to simply respond, "Hey, how are you? Sure, let's go out."

Believe it or not, this actually worked. I met a couple of girls that way, including one who was a little older than me and who I was together with for almost three years. During that time, I didn't have a car—I didn't have anything—so most of our dates were spent in the park together, talking, holding hands, kissing once in a while, or walking around the city. I could occasionally splurge on a movie, but more often than not, we were both happy to just be in each other's company.

Aside from learning about the opposite sex, I was also

undergoing a type of political awakening in the face of a changing Turkey. In the spring of 1950, Turkey had held its first truly independent and free election in its history, and even though I was just thirteen, I followed it closely, along with the rest of my family. Since the establishment of the Republic of Turkey in 1923, there had been a single party democracy, with the Republican People's Party (the CHP) at the helm. For a variety of reasons, over the next twenty-seven years of CHP dominance, the party had begun losing favor with constituents. One factor was that during World War II, the government had administered some severe cutbacks in social aid, which the people of Turkey never truly forgave them for, as these were difficult times not easily forgotten for the middle and lower classes.

Another party, the Democratic Party (the DP), was on the rise, and in the 1950 election secured close to 80 percent of the vote. The CHP was considered to be controlled by educated and experienced people, which some saw as the "elite," while the Democratic Party, with the exception of some very higher-ups, was formed by the middle class, and by 1950, the middle class had had enough.

DP supporters, including most of my family and me, criticized the CHP's many failures, and looked to the new party to fix some of these wrongs and continue modernizing the country. The DP promised real democracy, demolishing oppressive government forces and offering freedom for all. They vowed to stop and prosecute any unlawful business practices—such as bribery, kickbacks, and other widespread corruption—while also advocating for a completely free press. One of the major aspects of their platform was to improve the economy, get it back on track, and open up the country for trade and commerce, developing the nation to the levels of Europe or the US.

When the new prime minister, Adnan Menderes, was elected, he reinstated programs that had been dropped or underfunded during the war, and it seemed like the country was moving in the right direction. However, the DP also began a campaign for Muslim authority, a strong push to convince the country that the only "real Muslims" were DP party members. They had a more hard-lined approach too, which didn't fit well with many of the younger generation's more contemporary understanding of Islam and religion in general.

This uneasiness wasn't the only issue. By 1957, due to Prime Minister Menderes's spending, which had become a bit like that of a drunken sailor on leave, inflation started to shoot up dramatically. Now it was the CHP's chance to criticize their opponents harsher than ever. The DP also started performing very draconian, undemocratic actions, the opposite of what they had planned to do when they first gained power in 1950.

This all came to a head while I was living in Turkey, during the spring of 1960. At the beginning of May, students held a demonstration in the center of Istanbul. By that point, I wasn't a supporter of the CHP or the DP, but I also knew that something had to change or the country would be setting itself backward to a time before Ataturk's revolution, almost like the Dark Ages. As the demonstrations were underway, a fellow student from my hometown was badly wounded in the streets by the military. I couldn't stand by idly any longer, and the following day I joined with the other students to take to the streets as the universities throughout Istanbul were shut down.

As I marched with the crowd, I found a Turkish flag in the street. In a moment of patriotic fervor, for my country and my people—not just some political party—I took that flag and ran toward the main gate of the University of Istanbul, which was up ahead of us. Climbing up the gate, to cheers of approval, I hung the flag up high and jumped back down. I watched the white star and crescent undulate on their red background, reminding me of a well-known Turkish poem, one that speaks to the power and patriotism of the Turkish people. The poem states that the red of the flag represents the blood of our nation, which our countrymen sacrificed to unite Turkey into one state after World War I. I turned to the crowd and recited the poem. Having seen me take the first action, others joined in and started speaking as well—we now had a full-fledged political rally on our hands.

The students were going wild, the crowd having grown to thousands, shouting through the night, exchanging thoughts and hopes for the country's future. But a little past midnight, the military arrived with a fleet of trucks. Pandemonium erupted and many of the demonstrators scattered amidst the soldiers as they tried to corral us.

They managed to load many of us up, including some of my friends and me, and drove us to the military barracks on the outskirts of the city. There they held us in one large open area, with nowhere to sit except for the dirt floor.

Everyone was convinced that we were done for, swapping horror stories about our final fate—shot dead, hanged, starved—none of us knew what was going to happen. My memories of my run-in with the Syrian soldiers had always stayed with me, but hearing the students' stories I feared that the Syrian soldiers' brutality may have been nothing compared to what the Turkish soldiers were capable of.

The area where we were being held was not cordoned off by walls, bars, or fences, but there were soldiers surrounding us. I thought if I could sneak away from the group undetected, I could make a break for it. If I ran fast enough, the soldiers might not notice me until it was too late. I shared this plan with a few friends, and they all warned me that I would probably be shot in the back if I tried to escape.

I thought about it all night until the sun started coming up. My nerves were frazzled and I was exhausted, having not slept at all the previous night. I had screamed so much during the demonstration that I had lost my voice. But something about that sunrise reinvigorated me. As I looked out in the direction toward Istanbul, the city coming to life in the early morning light, I made my choice.

I've never run faster in my life. My exhaustion subsided

as adrenaline overtook me. I felt the muscles in my legs working to their fullest capacity, sweat pouring down my face and stinging my eyes. If any soldiers shouted after me, if any shots were fired, I have no idea. My focus was solely on running, blocking out everything around me— if a bullet ended my life, I wouldn't know anyhow.

After almost a half hour, I took a break and looked back. I couldn't believe how much distance I'd covered, the barracks far off. I stopped for a moment, out of breath and heaving, but not for long. The highway wasn't much further, so I started up again, though at a slower pace, and within fifteen minutes came to the side of the road. I was able to catch a bus and take it into the center of Istanbul, surely looking out of my mind, drenched in sweat, eyes bloodshot from lack of sleep, and my hair sticking out in all directions.

Instead of going to the dorms, I went to see Refik, who was working at an office in the city. He urged me to catch the first bus to Kilis as soon as possible. I didn't think the military was after me necessarily, but I was worried, maybe even paranoid. Little did I know that they had much bigger concerns.

I returned to my mother's house in Kilis, and she was so happy to have me there. For the next three weeks, I helped her around the house and in the fields, and was surprised to realize that in some ways, I missed that type of work. It was good to spend time with my mother as well, see my aunts and uncles—some who still stopped by almost every day—and catch up with the neighbors. Unfortunately, my mother often seemed tired. She was getting older but working almost as much, and as hard, as ever.

One day, after we'd gotten back from the vineyard, one of my neighbors came to our door, asking if we'd heard the news. Though my mother had electricity by then, she didn't have a radio, and I hadn't spoken with anyone all morning or afternoon. He told me that every station was announcing the same thing—the army had taken over the government in a full-on military coup. It was May 27, 1960, and the country would never again be the same.

A few nights later, people convened for a public meeting on the outskirts of Kilis to discuss everything that had transpired over the past few weeks. There were various opinions being touted, the pros and cons. I had been invited to come make a speech, as by then I was known in town as an educated young man from a good family, and word had spread that I'd been part of the student uprising.

Though my mother didn't want me to go, I accepted the invitation. When I arrived at the meeting, there were many other students there who had also fled Istanbul. Someone told me to go up to a podium that had been placed in the front of the audience, and before I could take my first step in that direction, I was hoisted up by crowd members and carried on their shoulders up to the front. I tried to express my points eloquently and powerfully, hoping to provide some insight as I saw it. I talked about the student uprising, how the demonstration began, and why we had undertaken such an action in the face of a government that was growing more oppressive and corrupt. I was rewarded with cheers and applause.

A few days later, the schools in Istanbul began reopening, and I returned to the city. Oddly, life pretty much went back to normal for me, though I had a sneaking suspicion that the students had been used by the newspapers, professors, and military leaders to their own ends, all of whom had profited from the coup. It seemed that everyone instrumental to the government, along with the media, our teachers, and the army's higher ups, were doing everything in their own self-interest, not for the betterment of Turkey.

The students had truly believed that we could make a difference in how things were run in the country. Instead, the aftermath was sickening, all the parties involved taking advantage of the situation. There was a tribunal held with the recently deposed members of the DP, who were put on trial as if it were a form of entertainment. Thousands of people from all around went to witness this spectacle, but I found it shameful, so I didn't attend. As a result of the military coup, the prime minister and two cabinet members were hanged, and Turkey was plunged into a system of multi-party chaos that would last for the next forty-two years.

Not only did the situation scare me, but my heart broke a little over the growing divisions in Turkey. I had fallen in love with Istanbul and was tempted to stay, but just as with the Syrian soldiers years before, I knew that if I didn't make a major change in my life, I might be risking my future. The violent military coup and Turkey's instability left me with little hope, so I began to consider my options after graduation, which was fast approaching.

Dogan's graduation at Technical University of Istanbul, Turkey, 1961.

Throughout college, I had continued to hear from Ihsan, who sent me letters almost once a week from America, where he had moved in 1957 after having successfully applied to ten hospitals in the US—no simple feat for a young Turkish man who knew absolutely no English. He actually had to have professors and other students who spoke English help him write his application letter and fill out all the forms. He had told me that if he had been able to complete the paperwork in Turkish, he probably would have gotten into more programs, but he was accepted by two, which was good enough.

His letters were beyond enthusiastic, sharing everything he was learning in, and about, the States. He thought it was the greatest place on Earth and could not praise it enough—how clean it was, how nice and accepting the people were, how young immigrants could truly make something of themselves there. "This America's unbelievable," he wrote, and he wanted me to join him as soon as I finished school.

He also knew how to entice a young man of my age, claiming that if I came and worked in the US, I'd be able to make money, buy the best car, and meet the most beautiful women. Really what he meant though was that I would have the freedom and ability to live a good life on my own terms, away from the fields and away from Turkey's turmoil. He knew how hard I had studied and worked to get to where I was, and he wanted me to continue toward a future we could both be proud of.

With the state of Turkey, and with no other immediate plans of my own, I began to mull the situation over. I was no longer dating the young woman I had met earlier in college, and it seemed that there were more opportunities for an engineer in the US than in Turkey. Similar to my brother, to become an engineer in the US I'd have to attend school while I worked, but I looked forward to this prospect. Ihsan said he'd be able to help me secure a visa, all I had to do was get into college. Just as he had, I asked a number of professors and friends who spoke English to help me with my applications.

Going to America had been a boyhood dream of mine. My interest had only been stoked by my brother's letters and encouragement, and by what I had heard about the country as I had gotten older. By the early '60s, I thought the United States was like some type of nirvana. It was beautiful—"from sea to shining sea"—and modern in a way that Turkey was not. People were friendly and welcoming. We saw American movies and heard about the country on the news, its power and sense of political, religious, and cultural freedom. It was a place for everyone and had everything anyone could ever want. For so long, it felt completely out of reach, and then my brother shattered that false notion.

I also didn't want my education to be in vain. My eyes had been opened in high school and college, and not just in the classroom, though I had learned plenty there. A rounded education shouldn't be taken for granted, as learning about a wide range of subjects creates a broader perspective and a better understanding of the surrounding world. There are so many people today who don't receive these opportunities, even in the US.

The US is actually falling behind many other industrialized nations when it comes to education—the system is underfunded and many colleges are cost prohibitive, either out of reach or destined to put students in debt for years to come. As a nation, we spend trillions on things like the military, but we can't find enough in the coffers to make sure children are being given a fair chance, an opportunity to succeed, the same as I was given in the 1940s in Turkey. When a society strongly supports education, everyone is given a chance, inequality diminishes, and an informed and educated population leads to a better world. If given the opportunity, it's astonishing what people can do.

Some of my experiences in Kilis and Istanbul may

have made me skeptical of authority, but I also found personal growth in confronting conflict and in relying on myself. College isn't just about classes and tests, either. It's also about learning how to interact with other people on different levels, whether for better or for worse, and developing a sense of empathy and understanding. I realized at that age that I didn't know everything, but I certainly knew a lot more than I had just a few years earlier. And with all of this knowledge and these new experiences under my belt, I felt I was ready to move forward. I hoped my time in the US would only further help me grow and that I could one day return to Turkey to give back to the country that had given so much to me.

I had applied to three or four schools, and the University of Maryland accepted me. I also got in to Stevens Institute of Technology in New Jersey, but my brother figured out a living situation for me near Washington, DC, so Maryland was the natural choice. There was also something about being in the nation's capital that drew me in. After I graduated in May of 1961, I worked for three months in a government office, saving up some money before I moved on to bigger and better things—a whole new life awaiting me, halfway across the world.

3

Welcome to the States

I HAD MIXED FEELINGS ABOUT leaving Turkey. On the one hand I felt prepared, ready to grasp this new opportunity, and on the other hand, I wasn't wholly sure what I was getting myself into. I hadn't left the country before, aside from going to Syria—and look how that had turned out— and I'd never been so far away from my family and home. I especially worried about my mother now that both my brother and I had flown the nest, and not everyone I knew thought this idea was as sound as Ihsan and I did.

People asked, "What's the point? Why can't you stay here and be an engineer in Istanbul or Ankara? Why America? Why *more* school? Turkey's not so bad."

I tried to explain my intentions and feelings, my personal goals, and my concerns about Turkey. I also fully believed I'd be coming back someday, and I assured everyone I spoke with that whatever I learned in the US would be put to good use in Turkey once I returned. I'm not sure if anyone believed that part of my plan—"Once you're gone, why come back?"—but when all was said and done, everyone wished me good luck.

While I had been deciding whether or not to go, I'd been speaking with Ihsan, who held an outsized influence on me, and I'm glad he did. With his support and my educational achievements, I was able to take this next step in my life, and as much as I wanted to do this for myself, I also wanted to make Ihsan, and the rest of my family, proud. Graduate school in America—I would have never thought it possible.

Still, I had my reservations. Moving to America wasn't without its own risks. I wasn't sure what I'd do if I failed, if my plans didn't turn out as I hoped and I had to fly home to Turkey with my tail between my legs. I didn't know how things worked in the US—the culture, the language, the geography—so I'd be facing a steep learning curve. I didn't speak English, I couldn't drive, the only person I knew there was my brother, and though I'd heard it was a welcoming country, how was I to know if that was true or not?

When I arrived in the US on November 21, 1961, I touched down on the tarmac at New York International Airport, Anderson Field, which most people called Idlewild, and which would later be renamed the John F. Kennedy International Airport. I was nervous, my palms moist and my knees shaking ever so lightly. As soon as I got off the plane, however, I felt reinvigorated. I looked around, watching people from all over the world arriving there in the US, and I knew I was right where I wanted to be.

I also knew I had a lot to learn, especially with school starting in January.

Not knowing the language was the first major hurdle I faced. My brother was so concerned about my lack of English that he had sent me a note to carry in my pocket in case I got lost when I arrived at the airport. All it said was, "I am going to New York, please help." I also had about one US dollar to my name; before I'd left Turkey, I had given my mother the rest of the money I'd saved up.

Luckily, Ihsan lived in Manhattan then, so he was able to pick me up at the airport, otherwise I would have been utterly confused and would have probably ended up on a bus to Connecticut, Pennsylvania, or some other state I'd not yet heard of. I couldn't read any of the signs at the airport, and I walked in circles until I found my way out of the terminal, where I waited for Ihsan. I had tried to memorize a few useful English words and phrases before I left Istanbul, but to little avail. The only one I could really remember was "Turkey," but if anyone had asked me where I was from, I wouldn't have had any idea what was being said, so knowing the name of my home country wasn't all that useful.

I was relieved when Ihsan pulled up to the curb, hopped out, and embraced me, both of us smiling ear to ear. "Welcome, welcome," he said in both Turkish and then English—I was already learning. I laughed getting into his car, thinking of how only ten years earlier we hadn't had a donkey to get around Kilis, and now my brother was about to drive me into New York City in his very own four-door sedan.

When we pulled out of the airport onto the highway, I was overwhelmed by the cars, trucks, vans, and motorcycles zipping along, some driving in our direction, others against traffic on the other side of the road, and still more in the overpasses above and the underpasses below. I was convinced the cars merging into our lane were destined to sideswipe us. I wasn't used to such an endless amount of vehicles converging on all those roadways. In Turkey, there were no highways like these, nor were there the immense bridges or high-rise buildings I saw off in the distance. It felt as if I was in some strange, sci-fi wonderland, all foreign and futuristic, especially as we entered the city.

Looking out at the skyscrapers, I couldn't believe I was there. My brother pointed out various buildings, and he explained how most of the city was laid out on a grid. Once we got off the highway, even more amazing to me than the surrounding structures were the people walking along the sidewalks—the most diverse crowd I'd ever seen—people of all kinds, colors, and creeds, living together in this massive place.

I started paying attention to street signs and the signs on the buildings and shop fronts. To my surprise, I kept seeing one of the two words I now knew in English repeated: Turkey. I thought I must be mistaken. I knew there were Turkish people in the US, but why was the word plastered everywhere around the city?

I turned to Ihsan and said, "Wait a minute. I know 'Turkey.' What's with all of these Turkey signs? Are all these people Turkish?"

He laughed aloud as we slowed to stop at a red light. "No, no, no," he said. "Turkey is a kind of bird too. The US holiday Thanksgiving is on Thursday, so everyone's buying turkey to celebrate." He briefly told me about the significance of the holiday, but I wasn't paying much attention, trying to wrap my head around my first homonym.

As we drove to the Catholic hospital in Harlem where he both worked and lived, we caught up for a while, but he could tell I was exhausted from the trip. I had flown from Turkey to Amsterdam, where I had had a seventeen-hour layover. Though I had to wait there in the airport for almost an entire day, I couldn't catch a wink of sleep—I was just too excited. When I got to the US, I was surprised I could keep my eyes open at all.

Since Ihsan was living in a small room at the hospital, he had arranged for me to stay with a friend of his in an apartment close by. Before he took me there, though, we stopped at the hospital so he could show me around and introduce me to the other doctors and nurses. I was impressed by how many people knew his name and how they seemed genuinely excited to meet me, his brother. He had to get back to work, so we went from there to his friend's apartment, a small one-bedroom walkup, and he told me to make myself at home. I sat down on the couch, listening to the traffic pass by in the streets below—and then I was out like a light.

Ihsan had gotten to know many people through his work at the hospital, including a family who insisted he and I go to their home in Jersey City for Thanksgiving.

So two days after I arrived, we drove from Harlem down through Manhattan, and I took in every single sight and sound that I could. Despite it being a holiday, the city was alive with throngs of people, and as we reached the Holland Tunnel, I was almost disappointed to be leaving, even for just the evening.

The family in Jersey City welcomed Ihsan and I into their house as if we were old friends, and they treated us to a holiday feast: mashed potatoes, stuffing, green beans, cranberry sauce, gravy, and, of course, turkey. They were by no means a rich family, but they offered everything to us freely and plentifully. I smiled along with their conversations, and Ihsan acted as my translator as we all made hand gestures together in an effort to communicate. I left with a full stomach and a warm feeling in my heart, amazed by how accommodating they'd been to me, a total stranger, from a country they probably couldn't locate on a map.

The day after Thanksgiving, my brother put me on a DC-bound bus. After having been reunited and enjoying our time together in New York, it was a somber parting, but I didn't have long to wallow in sadness—I had so much to do before I started school once again and learning an entirely foreign tongue was my primary concern. I bought a book on English that I began studying on the bus and realized I'd have to sign up for a language course as well.

Not only had Ihsan made friends in New York and New Jersey, but also in DC, which is how I ended up with a place to live while attending the University of Maryland. When he first arrived in the US, Ihsan interned at a hospital in DC where he was just as big of a hit as he was at the hospital in Harlem. While there, he met an elderly woman named Ms. Farachie who often came in complaining of all sorts of aches and pains. Though she did have some common health problems for her age, many others were imagined—she was something of a hypochondriac. Whether her issues were real or imagined, my brother felt for her, and they spoke with each other often.

Ms. Farachie worked in a federal government office, but she spent many of her days at the hospital with my brother and the other doctors. She was lonely and didn't have any family to count on, and Ihsan was new to the country, all of his family and friends in Turkey. They developed a bond, and after some time, she took to calling him "son" and in return he called her "mother."

When Ihsan left for New York, Ms. Farachie told him that if he ever needed anything, anything at all, he should call her, and she would do whatever she could to help. She was grateful for the attention he had given her and for how he had treated her with such kindness and care. When he found out I'd be coming to the US, Ihsan called in the favor. Not only would Ms. Farachie let me live at her home in Anacostia—a neighborhood in DC named after the Anacostia River, which the neighborhood lies east of—but she was also willing to essentially be my sponsor.

I needed an American citizen to fill out some paperwork, similar to a visa, stating that he or she would cover my housing and expenses as necessary when I arrived in the states. Thanks to my brother, Ms. Farachie handled the paperwork and gave me a place to stay. It was so kind of both Ihsan and her, and I appreciated her charity to no end, but living with her was not without its own obstacles.

First, I hadn't realized that I wouldn't have my own room in her home. She lived in a small apartment that was a bit of a mess—both inside and out—and there was only one bedroom. That meant I had to sleep out in the living room. I was a little disappointed when I learned about this arrangement, but that all changed when I saw a big boxy, black-and-white television set sitting in her living room—the first TV I'd ever seen. Surely I'd get the opportunity to enjoy this piece of entertainment I'd been hearing about for years. Instead, it became the bane of my existence.

Ms. Farachie loved that television, and she'd stay up to all hours of the night watching it. That meant I couldn't go to sleep until she was ready to go to bed as well. There were a number of nights that I pleaded with her, asking her if I could just open up the pull out couch and lie down, but she always ignored my requests. I would end up trying to sleep on the floor with the TV blaring until she called it a night—sometimes early the next morning—and I could get onto the couch and pass out.

The second problem was that Ms. Farachie—god bless her—was a talker. And I mean a talking machine. I don't want to poke fun—I assume her anxiousness came, in part, from her health issues—but she was constantly buzzing in my ear. She just couldn't stop. I of course smiled and responded the little I could, but if I'm being honest, she drove me a bit nuts. My major respite from her chatter was getting out of the apartment to go study English.

School was starting on January 15th, meaning I had about seven weeks to get the language down as much as I possibly could. It was an intense crash course, and I threw myself into it wholeheartedly. As planned, I signed up for an English class in DC, and my brother generously footed the bill. He knew how important it was to have a strong understanding of the language before starting school, where all of my classes would be in English.

I studied almost eighteen hours a day, whether I was at home, on the bus to the center of the city where I had class, or in class itself. Figuring out all of the tenses seemed futile at first, but I began to develop a strong basic knowledge of the language, though its complexity regularly tied my brain up in knots. It was a stressful month and a half, and more than once I questioned my ability to tackle this subject. Some days I felt that my decision to move to the US may have been made in haste, but my perseverance paid off come January when I started school.

The University of Maryland was almost two hours from Anacostia, but I went there every day, taking one bus downtown, and the other from downtown to the university. Though it was a four-hour round trip, I made the best use of it, and I studied both in the morning on the way there and in the evening on the way home.

My life as a grad student in the US surpassed all of my expectations, and I overcame my fears of the language barrier and the potential for failure. I had made it this far, so why couldn't I go further in my education and in my life? I took three courses my first semester, the classes mostly consisting of students who were regular American kids. They were all friendly, and the fact that I was from Turkey didn't seem to make much of a difference to any of them—it's almost as if they didn't really notice.

After school began, I found out that there were about ten or fifteen other Turkish students at the university, so we made a plan to all meet up together one day. As soon as I saw them, I told them, "I will not speak Turkish." They all laughed, unsure if I was being serious, but with persistence I made my point clear. I knew if I immediately began speaking Turkish with them, I'd set a bad precedent, creating a crutch on which I would inevitably rely. Instead, by always speaking in English, even with the other Turkish expats, I would force myself to learn and to improve. We saw each other often in the coming months, but not once did I speak a word of Turkish with them.

My English progressed by leaps and bounds, not only through my school work, but also through Ms. Farachie's constant talking: Who would have guessed? However, life with Ms. Farachie had begun to wear on me. Her television obsession hadn't subsided, and it was getting harder for me to deal with her schedule now that

I had to get up to catch the bus at 5:30 or 6:00 every morning. I also could never get any work done when she was around, as she always wanted to either chat or have me take care of things in the apartment. I didn't mind doing the dishes, taking out the trash, changing light bulbs, keeping the place clean, and the like, but at some point I needed to get to my studies, which I couldn't always do with her there. I had to concentrate on school—that was the whole reason I was in the US in the first place.

When I complained about this situation to one of my Turkish friends, he convinced me I needed to get out of there. Of course Ms. Farachie meant well, and the free room and board were unbeatable price wise, but I couldn't take it anymore. My friend told me he could help me find a room in a house a mile from campus, and within a few days, I was moving in. The rent was something like $20 a month, but I still needed help financially, so my brother said he'd be willing to cover the costs.

Ms. Farachie was not only disappointed that I moved out—she was angry. She showed up at my new home late one night to literally throw some of the things I had mistakenly left at her place in my face. She was ranting and raving, saying she'd sue me, and I felt horrible, trying to reason with her and explain my situation. Thankfully, in a few days, she stopped by again and apologized, and we actually kept in touch going forward. We would even get together occasionally. In many ways, she was my first friend in the US, and though she had her quirks and issues, I couldn't have started school without her, nor would my English have progressed so quickly.

I had also become friendly with a number of my professors, including my international student advisor, Dr. Bridges. He enjoyed hearing my stories about growing up in Turkey and was impressed with my performance in class and by how much my English had improved throughout the semester. Outside of school, he also helped put on various programs and events for local organizations.

One day he stopped me in the hall and said, "Mr. Uygur, if you are available, and so inclined, I'd like to take you some place this Saturday night to share your stories and knowledge of Turkey with the Baltimore Ladies' Association."

I was flattered by the invitation, but hesitant about speaking publicly in a language that I'd only been studying for a few months. Though my English had progressed, giving such a presentation would be a challenge; but I think that's exactly why Dr. Bridges had extended the invite.

The truth is, nothing is gained without embracing challenges, and I had been finding this more with every passing day in the US. I had come there to learn, to work, and to live life as I saw fit, trying out new things, meeting new, interesting people, and testing myself. Part of this ongoing test was to get out of my comfort zone, take advantage of new experiences, and develop insights that may have otherwise been unavailable. Small obstacles, like speaking in front of an audience, can be daunting, and life would be easier if they were avoided, but it would also be less fulfilling. I was honored that Dr. Bridges had thought of me and that he believed my thoughts and tales were worth sharing.

So in the spirit of taking risks and seizing the day, I figured why not, what was the worst that could happen? After being raised in Kilis, encountering the Syrian soldiers, living in Gaziantep alone when I was fifteen, going to college, surviving the protests and military coup, and moving to America, I felt that this would be a breeze, no matter my level of English. I have always found it helpful to consider past accomplishments and achievements when weighing the pros and cons of a current decision, comparing the more trivial problems to serious ones that I have had to deal with in the past. And if I've been able to make it through those serious ones unscathed, it seems that the smaller ones should be simple to navigate, no-brainers that should be welcomed.

I accepted Dr. Bridges's invitation and he picked me up that Saturday night. I wore my best suit—my only suit—and brought along a stack of notecards, my notes on them written in English. To a seated crowd of around 300 people, I delivered my speech, relaying some personal stories about growing up in Kilis, along with my experiences in Gaziantep and Istanbul. I especially enjoyed talking about the history of the country, Ataturk's revolution, and how Turkey was then developing. After I spoke, I was asked all sorts of questions about my life, Turkey, and Islam, and I was surprised by the crowd's genuine curiosity and attentiveness. To me, my life had been anything but exceptional; their questions and comments spoke otherwise. I felt a tinge of pride, and I was flattered that they'd taken such an interest in my life and my home country.

More than anything, I was over the moon about my ability to not only give the speech, but also answer all those follow-up questions, solely in English. Numerous people came up afterward to tell me how impressed they were with my command of the language and how enlightening the conversation had been. At that point, I was beaming, knowing I had just made a major stride in my life's plan. This experience also increased my confidence more than I would have ever expected, and in retrospect I think Dr. Bridges had known that would be the case all along. I thanked him and the rest of the audience for such a great evening.

After that night, I felt as if I was truly becoming part of my newly adopted home and country. I was a middle-class immigrant from Turkey, and I had been given a chance, not just by Dr. Bridges and the BLA group, but by the University of Maryland, the students in my classes, my landlady, my teachers, and everyone else around me, and so far, I was succeeding. For me, this was a sign of American democracy in action, that welcoming spirit of inclusion that I had heard so much about. I realize that the US wasn't perfect then by any means and not everyone was treated equally, the civil rights movement had only recently taken ahold, but I could see progress in America, whereas in Turkey I saw stagnation and even regression.

With Kennedy in the White House, there also seemed to be an air of hope for the future of the country—movement forward, not backward. While my brother and I had considered the US akin to Shangri-La, others in the international community had not been as enthralled by America in recent years. To some, the country had been saddled with an ugly, self-absorbed image characterized by an imperialist attitude, especially in regards to emerging nations in Africa and Asia. When Kennedy entered the White House in January of 1961, he set out on a crusade to erase that conception, what many Americans thought of as a misconception.

One of the ways he planned to do so was by backing the newly developed Peace Corps program, which he had first proposed as a congressman almost ten years earlier and then started with the signing of a March 1961 executive order after he became president. These volunteers went to almost every country to teach English and help others understand what Kennedy saw as true American ideals, the freedom and democracy that I and many of the other international students were searching for. Just as the DP had claimed in Turkey, Kennedy wanted to develop positive working relationships with the rest of the world. Unlike the DP, I thought Kennedy would see the idea through. I admired his leadership and resolve as he attempted to ingratiate America to the international community.

So when I received an invitation to the White House, I was dumbfounded.

The invite happened so casually. One day I went out to the mailbox to check if I had gotten any letters. I still heard from Ihsan often and from my other family members in Turkey. That day, though, I pulled out only one piece of mail, which had a return address that simply stated "The White House." I inspected the small envelope, noting the Project Mercury stamp in the upper right-hand corner. I assumed it was some type of joke or junk mail but I opened it up, my curiosity getting the best of me.

There on a piece of stiff almost cardboard-like paper, underneath a golden Great Seal featuring a bald eagle and the motto *e pluribus unum*, I read the following, written in an elegant cursive: "The President and Mrs. Kennedy request the pleasure of the company of Dogan M. Uygur at a reception to be held at The White House Thursday afternoon, May 10, 1962 at 3:30 o'clock."

I was speechless.

How was this possible? How would anyone at the White House know who I was, and why would the president of the United States of America want me to attend an event there? I figured somebody was pulling my leg, so I took the invitation to school the next day and asked some other students to take a look. Then I showed it to a few professors. Everyone agreed that it was the real deal—I had been invited to the White House by JFK.

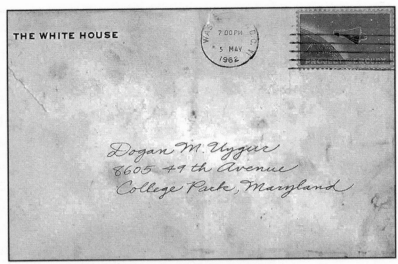

White House Invitation addressed to Dogan Uygur, 1962.

White House Invitation details, 1962.

In addition to the Peace Corps and other new programs Kennedy was trying to implement, he also wanted to reach out to the international community within the US, starting with all of the young people who came from overseas to study at the many universities around DC. Of course inviting international students to a reception at the White House was great PR—and it would inevitably create the type of "good feeling" that the Kennedy administration was hoping to garner—but I also saw it as an honest approach by the president to highlight the country's support of immigrants.

Among all of the colleges contacted about the reception, the University of Maryland had been included, and due to my background and educational performance, I made it onto the suggested list of invitees. In the back of my mind, I wondered if this was all real, but there was only one way to find out: I accepted the invitation and prepared for the big day. The only problem was that I had no way of getting there.

The White House is about forty-five minutes from the University of Maryland, but there was no direct public transportation to get there from where I lived. My lack of a car, a license, or any idea on how to drive there from Maryland put me in a predicament.

I told a few of the students in my program about my dilemma, hoping someone would be kind enough to offer me a suggestion on how to get there or, better yet, offer me a ride. It turns out having an invitation to the White House goes a long way—at least it did then, though I can't speak for today. Regardless, while I was discussing the issue, a student from one of my classes told me she had a car and that she would be happy to go with me—who would pass up such a trip?

A week later we were welcomed at the White House and led to the reception in the Rose Garden, which was packed. Students mingled together, many speaking English—some better than others—but also catching up in their native languages. It seemed like almost every country from around the globe was represented that afternoon, and I felt a sense of camaraderie among the assembled party. We were there because we had all taken a chance, a chance to see the world, to come out of our shells, and to succeed on our own. I was proud of being Turkish, of being an immigrant, but in that moment I was simply proud to be part of this larger group of people who were striving to make a better life for themselves.

I'd only been there for ten to fifteen minutes when all of a sudden, out of the blue, I came face to face with President John F. Kennedy himself. One minute I was lost in thought and the next I was shaking his hand, that charismatic smile on his face, showing off his pearly white teeth. In his well-known Massachusetts accent he asked me, "So wheeh ah you from?"

I was so surprised that, at first, I was unable to speak, but I managed to recover and say, "Turkey," to which he replied, "Oh, a great country." He then thanked me for coming and moved on to talk with the other students.

Though just a brief moment, it was astounding. I looked around me and up at the White House and thought, what a country, what a country.

I continued feeling that way as opportunities kept opening up to me. Though the '60s in the US weren't perfect, my experience speaks to the success of the country's international focus and welcoming attitude. Maybe the US wasn't heaven on earth, but, at times, it certainly seemed like it to me. Today, there's been a blunt reversal of this forward-thinking stance on immigration and on standing with the international community, and it breaks my heart. The US administration has gone in the face of everything the country once stood for, withdrawing from the UN Human Rights Council and the Paris Agreement, slapping tariffs on international products, and embracing insularity and isolationism. Worse yet, the treatment of immigrants has changed so drastically that I believe if JFK were alive today he might not recognize the country. At the time though, I was living in Kennedy's America, and after that day at the White House, I felt that nothing was out of reach for an immigrant like me.

Not long after, I heard from one of my uncles in Ankara who suggested I get in touch with one of his neighbor's sons, Adnan, who lived in DC. I enjoyed meeting new people, so I called him up one afternoon. Adnan had been expecting to hear from me and invited me to come to his home for dinner the following evening.

We chatted, in English of course, and it turned out that he ran the Turkish Department for the Voice of America, the US government-funded international radio broadcaster. Just as it does now, VOA programming widely influenced international public opinion about the US and its leaders during the '60s. It also shared interview segments with foreigners abroad. While we spoke over dinner, I explained how long I'd been in the country and my experience so far, and he suggested that he interview me for his show on VOA. As with all of the other opportunities presented to me while in the US, I couldn't turn it down.

That week he had me come to DC to the VOA headquarters, where he interviewed me for about a half hour, asking me all about my impressions of the US and my time spent there. The segment was transmitted in Istanbul, and a few weeks later I received a letter from one of my best friends who lived there. He wrote to tell me that he had actually heard my interview by chance one afternoon in Istanbul while listening to Voice of America—he could not believe his ears.

Maryland and DC had been a grand introduction to the country, and as the semester came to a close, I began thinking about what I was going to do that summer. In the fall, I would need to begin working during the day and attending class in the evenings, but I thought it would be best to make some extra money in my down time over the next few months.

A couple of my Turkish friends who had finished up their masters at the University of Maryland the prior year had come to visit, and they told me they were heading to New York City for work. Both of them were engineers and had some decent jobs lined up. Since I didn't have any plans and I needed a job too, I tagged along. I figured I'd be closer to my brother and maybe his friend would let me stay with him again. I realize that my plan was far from hashed out, but I was young and excited, riding high on my introduction to the US.

My brother was glad to see me and put me up with his friend again, but he told me to make sure I got busy and find a job soon. I didn't want to seem like a drain on anyone, so I immediately went to an employment agency when I got to the city. From the central agency downtown, they sent me out to a number of interviews throughout New York and then over into New Jersey. I didn't know much about the layout of either the city or New Jersey, but I figured out the bus routes, went on a number of interviews, and within two weeks I had landed a job as a mechanical engineer in a machine manufacturing company in Passaic, New Jersey.

Getting to New Jersey every morning from Harlem was a nightmare, and I felt that I'd already overstayed my welcome at my brother's friend's, so I started looking for a place to live in Passaic. I didn't have a car, so I had to make sure wherever I ended up wasn't far from my job. Luckily, I found a room for rent by a nice family whose house was about a mile and a half from work. They were the sweetest people, and, just as I had done with my host Ms. Farachie in DC, I helped them around the house as much as I could.

They were a devout Jewish family, but had no issues with my background, religious or otherwise. They even seemed to be happy to have a non-Jewish person in their house who could turn the lights on and off on Friday night and Saturday when they were observing the Sabbath. We all got along well, I enjoyed my new job, and I wasn't necessarily looking forward to going back to Maryland.

That's when Ihsan suggested that instead of returning to Maryland, I try transferring to the Stevens Institute of Technology for my remaining time in grad school. Well, why not? I thought. It was nice being closer to my brother. And if I went to Stevens, I could potentially work at Davidson Laboratory, a renowned research lab at the school. I filled out the application and all the paperwork—on my own—and I was accepted, both at school and to work in the lab. Stevens was in Hoboken, just over the Hudson from Manhattan, and the more I learned about the school's engineering program, the more I thought it was a better fit for me.

Once again, I had to move in order to be closer to work and school. I stopped in at the Stevens student center to ask if they knew of any potential housing opportunities, and I was told that a woman who lived on Bloomfield Street, not far away, was looking for someone to rent a room. After I found out where Bloomfield Street was, I went over to the house and introduced myself.

Like me, the landlady was an immigrant, but from Germany. She lived in the house with her American husband, and they were renting out one room, fully furnished with a bed, dresser, and a TV, all for a whopping $30 per month. I couldn't turn it down. Not only was the house within a five-minute walk of school, but Frank Sinatra's family lived in the house across the street in which he had grown up, which I got a real kick out of— everywhere I went in Hoboken those days, there were photos of him plastered up in every restaurant, corner store, and bar.

I started going to an international student center across the river in Manhattan where I met new friends with whom I attended conferences and went on group field trips with, learning more about US history and culture. A couple of Americans had started the International Student Center to welcome young immigrants to the US and provide them with learning opportunities and resources.

In addition to a group of Turkish students I met there, I was also introduced to many people from Europe and South America. Together, we were all studying English and learning about the US, but I learned about the parts of the world where they were all from as well—a wide world I had not yet seen. Being able to share stories and experiences in English, no matter our mother languages, was phenomenal.

The thing is, I could have just stayed in Turkey and not have done any of this. Even if I lived in Istanbul or moved to Ankara, I would have likely been able to find a decent job, keep my head down, and stay out of trouble. But when an opportunity presents itself, if not seized, it will likely be regretted later on. And sometimes it's necessary to create these opportunities. Risk is of course involved, but all good things in life require risk of one sort or another.

Proven by both my experiences in Turkey and my first year living in the US, it pays to ask people for help and guidance—more often than not, they'll give it to you. If

I hadn't asked, I would never have made it to the US in the first place, I wouldn't have had a place to live, and I wouldn't have received the many opportunities I had. Think about it: I wouldn't have been able to meet JFK if I hadn't asked someone for a ride! The smallest gestures can create the largest impacts.

Taking risks was the most important part to my growth. I was never reckless, and I always had a least *something* of a plan in mind, but if I hadn't put myself out there, I wouldn't have gotten anywhere. I ended up at Stevens, finished up my master's degree, and went on to work as a mechanical engineer in the research laboratory full-time after graduation as I had hoped.

The one mistake I made then was that I had applied to Columbia for my doctorate and got in, but I chickened out. There were a number of reasons why, one being that I worried if it didn't work out, I wouldn't be able to return to my job at Stevens, which I desperately needed. I regretted this mistake for many years, realizing that if I had followed my gut and risked a little bit harder, pushed myself a little bit further, it might have been worth it. But there was a lesson here as well: I told myself that anything I did going forward, I would do full on or not at all. Taking chances and accepting opportunities had gotten me far in my life, and I wasn't ready to stop yet.

My next plan involved returning to Turkey, but I first wanted to spend some more time at Stevens and the lab, saving up money and preparing for my next move. I'd become accustomed to life in the US—I'd even learned to drive and bought my first car, though this in itself was a little risky. It was a beat up old Chevy that my boss at Davidson was trying to get rid of, and he sold it to me for $75 in the Stevens parking lot. I neglected to mention to him that I didn't know how to drive, but I just couldn't pass it up. A colleague and good friend of mine, who I still keep in touch with today, Bob Madden, gave me some driving lessons, and though they weren't a total disaster, I did need some practice to get a hang of it.

One night as we were driving through Hoboken, him coaching me along, he told me to take a right, but I misunderstood him at first. When I realized what he was saying, I turned sharply, ending up partially on the sidewalk. A second later, the flashing lights of a police car appeared behind us. I didn't have a driver's license yet—or a permit—so it took some explaining, but Bob saved the day. He told the officer that we were both students at Stevens and that as a recent immigrant, I didn't know how to drive, so he was giving me lessons. The cop was not amused, but told us to get out of there. We laughed together as I pulled off the curb and rumbled down the dark streets.

Life was moving along just as I'd hoped, so much so that I was unprepared for the next obstacle with which I would be presented: I received a telegram one day from a family member in Kilis. It looked like I'd be returning to Turkey sooner than I had planned, not to stay for long, but long enough to bury my mother.

4

Sharing the American Experience

I'D ONLY BEEN BACK TO Turkey once since I had moved to America, right after I had received my master's. I went at the tail end of a trip in which I had travelled to Europe, a special treat to myself for graduating. I went to London, Paris, and Rome, hitting all the major sights, like Buckingham Palace, the Louvre, and the Coliseum. It was an invigorating, and somewhat surreal, adventure, visiting all of these breathtaking places in person that I had read so much about over the years.

When I got to Turkey, however, it was a somber occasion. My mother's health was obviously in decline, and I could tell the twilight of her life was upon her. A few months after I returned to New Jersey, I received the telegram—she had fallen ill and needed to be hospitalized. I wasn't surprised, but it hurt just the same.

Though Kilis had been growing since I had moved to the US, the type of care my mother needed was not available in my hometown. She was taken to a well-respected hospital in Gaziantep, called American

Hospital, which had a long history in the area, having been established by missionaries in the 1800s. A week or two after I arrived, the doctors said she'd be better off in Ankara, where there was a hospital that specialized in the kind of kidney problems she was experiencing.

After checking her in to the hospital in Ankara, I stayed with an uncle who lived nearby so I could be close to her. Unfortunately, the doctors said there wasn't much they could do. Though it was a melancholy affair, I wouldn't trade the time I spent with her then for anything. I visited every morning and sat with her throughout the afternoon and into the night. When she was awake, we would reminisce together, and many of our friends and family from around Ankara came to see her, always lightening her mood. Her younger sister, my Aunt Munire, visited often, which was such a comfort to both my mother and I.

Though she became quieter with each passing day, a small smile always stayed on her face, looking at her young boy who had gone out into the world and returned to her as a young man. I like to think she was happy then, finally getting some well-deserved rest. She had lived a hard life, but a good one. Within a month after my arrival, come the end of October, she passed away, falling into a sound sleep while surrounded by people whom she loved and who loved her in return.

Even though I knew this was inevitable, seeing her go affected me in a way that I had never felt before and have never experienced since. In all of my eighty-one years, that pain was the most excruciating I've ever felt, and I wouldn't wish it upon my worst enemy. I distinctly remember the hour, minute, and second when it happened, and every time I think of it, a particular sense of sadness descends over me, if only momentarily.

I took her body home to Kilis where my family and I held a memorial service and funeral. A seemingly never-ending procession of relatives and friends from Gaziantep, Ankara, Istanbul, and abroad came to pay their respects. Everyone who arrived—neighbors, farmers, shopkeepers, cousins, uncles, aunts—all had stories about what an amazing person my mother was and how she had affected them in some way or another. It occurred to me then just how many lives she had touched and how important she had been to so many people.

We openly wept together as she was placed into the ground, and her funeral was performed in accordance with Islamic tradition, which meant that a fourteen-day mourning period followed, during which we had the chance to celebrate her life and lasting legacy. Afterward, I planned to stay in Kilis for a little longer to help make sure everything was in order before I returned to the US. One of my cousins had power of attorney, so he'd be taking care of selling the house and patches of land, but I wanted to go through the old family home one last time. I also just felt like I needed some more time there to process the situation, to visit with friends and family, and, in a way, reconnect with Turkey.

The country seemed to have stabilized somewhat since I'd been gone, though there was a sense of potential turmoil always afoot. Most people I spoke with, however, had high hopes for Turkey's future and many suggested that I move back to take advantage of the changing country.

I mentioned to a few people that I had actually been considering it at some point, and being in Turkey made me think about the idea more seriously. From as early on as I could remember, there had been an ongoing conversation about how Turkey was failing to develop industries like those in America and Europe. Many were convinced that Turkey was simply backward and would never be able to build up and become rich like other developing nations. I thought this notion was ridiculous.

Turkey had given so many of its people so many opportunities—I was living proof of that success—and I knew the time would come when it would be my turn to give back to the country. What I really thought Turkey could use was its own manufacturing industry, which was majorly lacking. Though development was taking place while I was living in America, most people in Turkey were still suspicious of locally manufactured machinery, thinking it was garbage that didn't work properly. If Turkey were able to build reliable production machinery, however, an entire new industry could emerge. Aside from my mother's death, this was the main thing on my mind as my days in Kilis came to a close, but unbeknown to me, the rest of my family thought I should be concentrating on something else entirely.

One morning while going through my mother's house—cleaning and organizing all of her possessions— my cousin's wife, Aliye, arrived at the door. I welcomed her in and we chatted for a while as she gave me her condolences once again over my mother's passing.

Then she said, "Well, now's as good time as ever."

"For what?" I asked.

"You know what," she said.

And I did—I assumed she was talking about something that she'd brought up to me more than once in the recent past: marriage.

Aliye had been insisting that I marry a "blue-blooded Kilis girl" ever since a scandal boiled over in my family a few years earlier when my brother married an American woman. It wasn't that Ihsan had anything against marrying a woman from Turkey, or Kilis in particular, but he hadn't come back to Turkey since moving to the US due to a visa issue; so even if he'd wanted to meet a woman in our hometown, he wouldn't have been able to. Instead, he met a wonderful woman named Patricia while he was working and living in Manhattan. He and Pat, as we call her, went on to get married, move to New Jersey, and have four children together, three sons and one daughter. Aliye had other plans for me, and it turned out she wasn't the only one.

In no time at all, my relatives stormed me: "Your brother got married to an American girl, and if you go back to the US now without a wife, you're going to marry one too. We're not going to let you do it!"

Though their words were half in jest, they did truly want me to marry someone from our hometown, maintaining my connection with the community despite living 5,000 miles away. In many regards, I was touched: they were looking out for my best interest while also trying to keep me inextricably linked to the family, friends, and place I had grown up in, one that had influenced me so strongly and led me to who I'd become.

I also had no objection to a traditional arranged marriage. I think I would have been just as happy meeting a woman in America, but while I was there in Turkey, among friends and family, listening to their thoughts and advice, and enjoying many things that I missed about the country, it seemed to all make sense. That said, I only had ten days until I needed to return to the US and my job at Stevens.

Especially for westerners, arranged marriages hold a type of stigma that, being born and raised in Turkey, I never thought much about. Even within the Turkish culture, some reject arranged marriages, but for me, it just wasn't a problem. And in the end, it's how I found my beautiful wife, Nukhet, who I have been married to for the past fifty-four years and with whom I raised two brilliant kids. Still, I can understand how people may have a knee-jerk aversion to this tradition.

One thing to know is that there is usually some type of social connection between the bride and groom, whether through their friends, families, or both. It's not as if two arbitrary people are simply thrown together one day without any say in the matter and that's that.

Typically, the family of the potential husband plans a small get together with the family of the potential wife. When the man and his family arrive at the prospective in-laws' home, everyone drinks coffee and tea and makes small talk. In lieu of dating or a prolonged courtship, this is a chance to get to know each other a bit better, both the families and the couple. If all goes well, and the couple can picture themselves together, plans are made from there. If the get together doesn't work out, and the relationship seems like it won't be amicable, then the two go their separate ways and try again with other possible partners and families.

For me, the process was truncated as I had to be back in New Jersey in less than a week and a half. I know it sounds rushed, to say the least, but if it hadn't gone just as such, I would have never met the love of my life.

I was introduced to three women, and of the three, Nukhet, caught my eye. It would be a lie to say looks didn't play a role, they certainly did—she was, and still is, gorgeous—but she was also warm, kind, and intelligent.

I had always hoped that I would spend my life with a woman who had been brought up to believe in similar ideals as myself: the importance of family and education, a progressive attitude, an aspirational mindset, and a belief in raising children in a way that would provide them with more opportunities than we had had growing up—I found all of this in Nukhet. She was smart, educated, and accomplished—a graduate of a woman's institute in Turkey where she had studied art and fashion—and she was excited about starting a family.

One of my cousins and one of Nukhet's cousins were best friends, almost like brothers, and other members of our families had known each other for a long time, so they were all integral in bringing us together. Still, this marriage was somewhat atypical because Nukhet's family was one of the wealthier ones in Kilis, whereas mine was not. Her grandfather had been the mayor, and the family held property in the southern part of town. Though Nukhet's father owned and managed this land, along with a sizeable number of workers, he became a dentist, a highly respected profession. He was also the only dentist in Kilis then.

Nukhet's father didn't just own a few disparate plots of land, either. He owned large tracts, some of which had been in the family for multiple generations, as early as the 1690s. We actually have an original "foundation document," signed and sealed in 1693, that outlines the ownership of a piece of land south of Kilis by one of Nukhet's relatives, Yavasca Suleyman Celebi. Suleyman Celebi had worked for the Ottoman state and, as was common, received the land as a retirement payment when he left the service of the Ottoman Empire.

Interestingly, the surname Yavasca can be traced back even earlier than the 1690s, leading all the way to Yavasca Shahin Pasha. Originally from Crimea, Shahin Pasha had been the Admiral of the Ottoman Navy when the Ottomans conquered Istanbul, then called Constantinople, in 1453, which led to the establishment of the Ottoman Empire. During this battle, Shahin Pasha devised an inventive way to attack the city. The Byzantines had blocked off the Golden Horn waterway, which leads from the Marmara Sea right into the center of Istanbul, with a giant chain so no unauthorized ships could come through. Shahin Pasha decided to get around this obstruction by building ships in the hills above the city, in an area now known as Levent. Today, Levent is one of the main business districts of Istanbul, but in 1453 it was just a forest.

Shahin Pasha and his men built these ships using the surrounding trees, then created a system of logs that ran down the hillside into the Golden Horn. They slicked olive oil on the logs and sent the ships careening down into the water. From there they attacked, conquering the city, and Shahin Pasha emerged as an Ottoman hero.

Nukhet's family's last name is Yavasca, and most of her family members have Crimean features, exhibiting a strong, long bloodline that connects to those early relatives. I found this more than 500-year history of the Yavasca family in southern Turkey impressive, but also daunting—why would Nukhet's family allow someone with my background to marry her?

Thankfully, in addition to the connections between our families, Turkey had been changing over the past decade and a half. Previous to 1950, Nukhet's and my relationship would have likely never come together, but after 1950— and the introduction of a more true form of democracy in Turkey—social barriers and stratification had started to crumble. Opportunities for social advancement and progressive ideals were growing. In addition, the access to free education that I had received put me on a more level playing field with people my age who came from the upper classes. If I hadn't received that education, I know for sure Nukhet's family would have never looked twice at me. But with these educational opportunities, more people were beginning to mix between social classes, their backgrounds having become less important to their current standings.

I was also able to cross this class divide because of my good reputation among our families and friends and my profession in the US. Being a mechanical engineer, living in the states, and owning a car all went a long way in showing that I had become a success since leaving Kilis as a young farmer. It also didn't hurt that Nukhet's mother, Ulker, had been hearing about me from her friends and family in Istanbul—a pure coincidence, but one that certainly worked to my advantage.

After living with my cousin Refik, his wife, Nigar, and my Aunt Hatice, I had stayed in touch with them. They had been impressed by my move to the US and my continuing education, and apparently they spoke of me often. One of Nukhet's aunts lived in Istanbul as well and was friends with Nigar. They would get together about once a month with a group of other women, and Nukhet's mother joined them one afternoon. During their conversation, my name came up repeatedly, and thank god Nigar had such a high opinion of me.

She told everyone that I was hardworking, clever, always willing to help out with the kids when I lived with her and Refik, and that I was excelling at graduate school in the US—all things a potential mother-in-law would want to hear about a prospective son-in-law. At that time, however, no marriage plans had been in the works, and Ulker didn't remember my name until my family approached her about taking her daughter's hand in marriage a few years later.

Though I was excited, not everyone in my family believed that these connections and societal changes were enough for Nukhet's parents to consider me an appropriate partner for their daughter. Some said not to approach Nukhet's family at all because of the difference in classes, thinking the results could have potentially been disastrous, embarrassing our family's name.

"They're going to say our family's too low. The wealthy marry among themselves," they told me.

But Aliye was convinced that I had a chance, as were a number of my aunts and other family members. Unfortunately, the initial meeting to discuss this possibility did not go as smooth as hoped.

The day Aliye and my aunts approached Nukhet's family to find out if her mother would be amicable to this relationship, they arrived just as Ulker was walking out of the house on her way to visit a friend. (In the arranged marriage process, the mother of the potential bride is always approached before the father.) They exchanged greetings and pleasantries, but then my family quickly got down to business, explaining why they had come to speak with her. In the process, they mentioned that I was only in the country for about a week more before I had to return to America, so time was of the essence.

Normally in such a situation, if the mother assents, she'd invite the family into her home to further discuss the possibilities of marriage—Ulker did no such thing.

Instead, she explained that she had mistakenly locked the key to the house inside.

"Well, how will you get back in later today?" one of my aunts asked, feeling that they were being given the runaround.

"Oh, well Nukhet has a key, and she'll be home before I will. My apologies," she continued, "otherwise I'd be happy to invite you in." And with that, she left.

My family got together that evening, and Aliye relayed what had happened. Most everyone agreed that Nukhet's mother simply wasn't interested and had told them a bald-faced lie—who locks their keys inside the house? They were all convinced she must have had the key but had refused to entertain the marriage. (Little did we know, my future mother-in-law locked herself out of the house often.)

Aliye just couldn't believe it, and she refused to give up that easily. She insisted we return. "I'm going back tomorrow," she said, "and I'm going to make this happen!"

The next day she called Nukhet's family and scheduled for all of us to meet at Nukhet's uncle's home, which we hoped wouldn't be conveniently locked as well. I went along with my closest family members, and when we arrived we were met by almost all of Nukhet's. I was intimidated and nervous, but when I saw her, sitting there smiling and welcoming me into her home, I felt something inside of me shift. A cloud of sorrow had been following me around ever since my mother's death, but in that moment it dissipated. Later on in life, Nukhet told me that meeting me that day had been love at first sight, that she had seen some type of light—daresay a sign—shining around me, like my aura. I felt the same, knowing then that I would spend the rest of my life with her.

Everyone talked together, enjoying the opportunity to catch up and discuss the match they were attempting to make. Nukhet's aunt asked me all sorts of questions, drilling me about the US, my job, my education, and nearly everything in between—how much money I made, whether or not I had a car—it was like being interrogated. Regardless, I didn't mind since I had good answers to all of her questions. During the conversation, Ulker realized that I was the Dogan she'd been hearing so much about in Istanbul from Nigar, and at that point she warmed to me quickly. Luckily, my reputation preceded me.

As standard, we had coffee and tea, and in a short time plans for the wedding were being discussed.

It was a small but official affair in Kilis, a modest ceremony and reception with our relatives and close friends. There was music and dancing, and everyone celebrated together before I unfortunately had to leave my new bride a few days later. Nukhet would be joining me in New Jersey soon enough, but I had been gone from work for weeks and needed to return. I also wanted to make sure I was ready for her arrival, keeping in mind she wouldn't be alone—her mother would be coming with her to stay with us for a few months as Nukhet got adjusted, and possibly to confirm that I was as good of a guy as advertised.

I hoped that I could show both Nukhet and Ulker how successful I'd become in America. I pictured them coming to the US, to "our home"—a phrase I often repeated to myself with excitement—and immediately realized that I could provide for Nukhet as promised. Nukhet had hesitations about coming to the US, knowing little about the country, so I wanted her to feel comfortable and pleased with her decision as soon as she got there. I also wanted to be the best husband possible, just as I knew I could be.

When I got back to the US, the first thing I did was move out of the small room I had been renting and found a nice apartment in North Bergen, New Jersey, just off of Route 3 near the Lincoln Tunnel. I also decided I'd try to keep myself busy and make some additional money. I had a purpose now that I hadn't had before, one that would push me forward to always do more and do better. I'd soon be starting a family, building a life with someone special, so I needed to save some money; it was worth it for me to do whatever I could. I thought that with a little ingenuity I could always find a way to make an extra buck, and so I stayed on the lookout for opportunities to supplement my income.

One evening I saw an advertisement in the newspaper that offered a chance to "make a lot of money," stating "*anyone* welcome to apply." The details were scant—the ad didn't mention what was being made, bought, or sold—but later in the week the company was holding an open house at their offices where potential employees could come meet, have a drink, and learn about the job. It all seemed a little fishy to me, and though it was in another part of New Jersey, I figured, why not see what happens?

As I drove out there, I quietly wondered if I was wasting my time. When I pulled into the parking lot of the building, I almost didn't go inside, but my curiosity lingered, so I got out of my car and walked in. I entered a room where ten or fifteen people were milling about, some younger than me, some older, all who looked like they could use a job.

After a few minutes, I realized the company sold pots and pans door to door and the ad had been for salesmen. I didn't feel above the work, but I asked myself what kind of engineer moonlights as a door-to-door salesman—not this one I thought. I was about to leave when the manager stopped me and said, "Just stick around for the presentation. You came all this way. Come on, just listen to what we have to say."

He got up in front of the audience and explained the process—which was exactly what I had expected—and presented a script of how to speak to potential buyers. I couldn't picture myself hawking cookware to strangers at their homes, but the manager got my attention when he started talking about how much money we could potentially make. He also explained that upon our first sale, we would get to keep the sample set. I thought this might impress Nukhet, though I still wasn't sure if it would be worth it. Somehow, though, the manager convinced me, and I left there with a giant, clanking suitcase full of pots and pans.

The manager paired me up with a salesman from Hoboken who took me out on a few runs to show me the ropes. He had the whole thing down pat: his clothes, his pitch, his facial expressions. He sold a few sets while I was with him, and he acted as if it was no big deal. After that day, he told me, "Okay, you're on your own buddy," and at that point I thought I could easily pick up where he had left off. So for the next month, every night after working at Davidson, I went door to door in the neighborhood, lugging that suitcase from my car up to unsuspecting homeowners' houses and then back to my car again. I gave the spiel the manager had suggested and tried my best to seem enthusiastic over what I had to offer.

I sold exactly zero sets that first month.

After everything I'd been through in the last ten, fifteen years, and all of the strides I'd made, I was having trouble selling some damn cookware to suburban moms. I actually started getting a bit resentful and decided to revise my approach in hopes of putting some sales in the books. I thought if I just got one, I'd be off to the races.

In addition to weeknights, I decided to try selling on Saturdays and Sundays. When I told the manager my plan, he said it wouldn't work: "Don't bother anyone on the weekends, they're not gonna buy anything off ya' then."

Well, I decided not to listen to him. That Saturday, after failing the night before to sell anything once again, I got up early and started my rounds, making sure not to stop at any houses I'd already tried. Just as with the previous evening—and the one before that, and the one before that, going back the entire month—no one bit.

Then, about halfway through the day, when I was

on the verge of giving up, I came to a house I had yet to hit on my route. It looked like all the other homes in the neighborhood, nothing special, and I didn't have a great feeling about my prospects. I just did as I had with all of the other houses: took a deep breath, dragged my suitcase up to the door, and rang the bell.

A woman appeared and I launched into my pitch, but before I was halfway through, she stopped me and screamed into the house up a staircase, "Mary! There's a pots and pans man here. Come down!"

The woman invited me in and introduced me to her daughter, Mary, who rushed down from upstairs. It turned out Mary had graduated from high school that year and would be getting married soon. She had planned on buying cookware anyhow, so she and her mother were both pleased to see me, which was a new experience for me as a salesman. She told me to write up an order, and with that I made my first sale.

As promised, I got to keep the sample pots and pans from the first sale I made, a set that Nukhet and I have to this day. From then on, wherever I went, I just sold, sold, and sold some more, at least two to three sets per week. For whatever reason, it became so much easier. One night I went to a house in Jersey City, around 6:30, and the young woman who lived there happened to have a group of classmates staying the night—every one of them bought a set. It only took an hour or two and my commission for that sale was about $600.

We had a group sales meeting every week, and when I told the manager about that previous week's sales, he was over the moon. He got up in front of the whole sales team and said, "Look at this guy. He barely speaks English, and he sold three sets to *one* house. You guys were all born here! How the hell can't you push this stuff like he can?" I begged to differ about my English—it was quite good by then—but he made a colorful point, and I was happy to be held up as a model example.

In many ways, I think the main reason my sales started to take off is that my self-confidence increased with my first success, and from then on I projected self-confidence when speaking with potential buyers. Just one small accomplishment can boost self-confidence and create a positive mindset of success. After my first sale, I knew I could do it, all I had to do was follow through, so I did.

I also simply enjoyed making sales—it was so different than my normal work. I was surprised that I had a knack for it, which made me enjoy it all the more. Self-confidence and inspiration can come from the strangest places, and I found that taking on an unexpected challenge was rewarding in its own right. I was trying something new that I thought would be boring and beneath me, but I actually liked it and looked forward to making each sale.

The manager was so pleased by my performance that he invited me to a conference in Pennsylvania. I reminded him that this was just a part-time job for me and I didn't plan to stick around for too long, but he insisted that I come. He and his wife picked me up in a big Cadillac and we drove to Philadelphia. I didn't know he'd be speaking to an audience of hundreds, nor did I have any idea that he would introduce me to the crowd, who applauded loudly. He talked about my background and my achievements as a salesman, which I appreciated, but I also thought it was kind of funny considering that this was by no means my career. After that night, he began nagging me to come on full time, and though I was flattered, I started getting a little tired of the job, and I worried that I'd be getting off course if I stuck around any longer.

I left and decided I could earn extra money by tutoring kids in middle school and high school. I took an ad out in the paper, "All science and math courses, all levels," and I received a number of calls, followed by referrals. For seven bucks an hour, I taught these kids mathematics, physics, chemistry, and any other related subject. And though it may not seem like much, seven dollars an hour then wasn't so bad, though it was nothing like the money I made with the cookware. Regardless, every bit helped, and I had been storing up a nice little nest egg for Nukhet and I once she arrived. But, her arrival seemed to be taking forever.

While I was in Turkey, I had gotten copies of the paperwork that showed we were officially married, and so when I came back to the US I applied for Nukhet's visa. I had to translate the paperwork into English and then send it along to the US immigration office. I figured it wouldn't take long, but then I waited. And waited. And then waited some more. After almost six months, I hadn't heard anything.

Then, one day, I was talking to my sister-in-law, Pat,

and I told her about the situation. "I don't know what happened," I said. "I translated the Turkish paperwork, filled out the application, sent in all the appropriate forms, and I still don't know what's going on. No one has contacted me, my wife, or her family."

Pat asked, "Why don't you write a letter to your senator?"

"What would be the point?" I said. "The senator doesn't know me from Adam. Why would he help me?"

"Oh, Dogan," she said, "No, no, no. In this country, if you write a good letter, the government will help you."

I wasn't so sure, but I didn't have any other options. So, I sat down and wrote a letter explaining the situation. I mentioned how I was studying thermodynamics and was actually working on a government research project for the US Army at Davidson, testing hydroplaning on military airplane tires. I also explained that without my wife in the US, I was having trouble performing my job, her absence affected me that much.

This was all true—I wasn't exaggerating. Ever since I had met Nukhet, she was constantly on my mind. My responsibilities had shifted, and everything I did in the US I was doing for her and our future together. She was to be my anchor, and we were to act as a source of inspiration to, and mutual care for, one another; without her, I was starting to feel lost and disillusioned. I could tutor kids, sell as many pots and pans as humanly possible, or find other extra work, but it wasn't the same. I had found the person I would share the rest of my life with, through thick and thin. I'd come a long way in the preceding years, but our marriage was the most important thing to have happened to me in my adult life. Without my wife by my side, however, were any of my accomplishments worthwhile?

I sent the letter and hoped for the best.

Less than a month later, the consulate in Adana, a city in southern Turkey about 100 miles from Kilis, contacted my wife's family. They told them Nukhet would be given a visa, but she had to first get her passport. Shortly thereafter, she and her mother flew to the US to join me.

Though we had had a ceremony in Turkey, we decided to have an informal wedding in the US as well. We got about ten friends together, including Ihsan and Pat, who came in from Dover, New Jersey, and spent a lovely afternoon together welcoming Nukhet to America. She was a bit shy, somewhat uneasy in a new country, and she knew she had many obstacles before her, just like I had when I first came to America, starting with learning the language. That said, I was there for her and she was there for me.

One morning, not long after she and Ulker had arrived, Nukhet was looking through one of the closets, hanging up some clothes, and she came across a gray and white jacket of mine. I'd had it since college when I had worn it often—it was considered stylish and distinct when I bought it—but it had been a while since I'd put it on.

I heard Nukhet gasp. "Where'd you get this?" she asked, pulling the old jacket from the closet.

"Back in Turkey," I said, "when I was a student in Istanbul."

"Oh, my god," she said, her eyes wide, a large grin on her face.

"What?" I asked.

"You were that guy."

"What guy?" I said, starting to smile myself. "What are you talking about?"

"The guy at the rally in Kilis, after the coup! I was there."

I had completely forgotten that when I had made my speech on the outskirts of Kilis in the spring of 1960, when I was carried on the shoulders of the crowd to the podium, I had been wearing that very jacket. We laughed over the coincidence, and though I'm not sure how much it played a role, starting that day she seemed to look at me a bit different, almost with a sense of admiration.

We fell into a beautiful life together, and we got along perfectly. I helped her with her English; she helped me with the house. I took her to New York City; she held my hand as we walked through Manhattan. In addition to her schooling in Turkey, she had also learned about what was called "home management" then—essentially "homemaking"—which came in handy once we had our children . . . and for me as well—sometimes I can be a big kid myself. There was a sense of the unknown and uncertainty in all of this, but our relationship developed smoothly and our bond grew stronger.

Though we were a match made in Kilis, I honestly felt that we were a match made in Heaven. I wanted to show

Nukhet everything I could in the US and have her share in the wonderful experiences I had been having since moving there. I bought a brand new car, a red Chevrolet Corvair, and I paid for it in cold, hard cash—$2,100, all of which I'd made from tutoring and selling those pots and pans. I was so proud that day, and Nukhet and I spent many following Sunday afternoons driving around New Jersey together, going on small trips in the area. We had such fun, I thought it might be nice to go on a longer road trip, somewhere out west or down south.

At Stevens, I saw a notice on a bulletin board about a program offering young foreign students and staff the opportunity to go on vacation to places throughout the country. The program set them up with families who would act as hosts for short periods. I looked into the program, and all I really had to do was pick a place to go and they'd try to accommodate us. I spoke with Nukhet and we decided on Miami, a place she had heard a great deal about and was interested in visiting.

When the Thanksgiving holiday rolled around, we packed up the Corvair and drove south, my young bride and I cruising down the coast to Florida. The drive alone was something else—seeing parts of the country we barely knew about—but we weren't prepared for the accommodations we'd have once we got there. We stayed with a successful architect and his wife, who were apparently well off based on their massive estate. Behind the main house, they set us up in a guesthouse, which was posh in its own right.

For Thanksgiving dinner, we went to a well-to-do

lawyer's who treated us to an incredible dinner. He and his wife both exuded wealth—he with an English style pipe in hand, she wearing a long dinner gown—but they both accepted us without question. I shared stories about my first Thanksgiving in the US and about misunderstanding the "Turkey" signs all over Manhattan—we all laughed together. After dinner, they brought out a plate of all kinds of cheese, some I had never even heard of before. I quietly asked Nukhet, "Why are they putting out cheese now? I'm stuffed."

I'm not sure if they heard me, but they explained how in some places cheese is traditionally eaten after dinner in order to help digestion. This was news to me, and though I was full to the gills, I had my fair share, as we all continued to chat and enjoy each other's company and entertainment late into the night.

It didn't matter that we were Muslim, or foreign, or that our English wasn't perfect: these people accepted us for who we were, understanding that we were just like everyone else in the US, whether American born or foreign born, striving to make a good life for ourselves and hoping to raise a happy, healthy family. This was long before the terms "Muslim" or "Islam" became so horribly interlinked with a popular American conception of terrorism. It was also before a time when immigrants were so vilified by heads of state in the US. Nukhet and I never experienced any anti-Muslim or anti-immigrant sentiments. Not to say that they didn't exist, but they weren't as widespread and insidious as today. My belief in America as a haven, and a heaven, as the greatest country on Earth, was so strong then.

I felt fortunate beyond my wildest dreams, living in the US with my wonderful wife. The plan I had set out in the fields of Kilis had become a reality, and I now wondered what was next. Though I loved America, ever since the last time I had been in Turkey, I kept considering returning. It got to the point where I couldn't stop thinking of the country, as if it were calling to me. Though Turkey had made some progress, I felt as if the nation Ataturk had hoped for, worked for, and fought for had not yet been realized. Instead of constant progression, Turkish industry, and in some regards society, was lagging. Once again, I thought about everything the country had given me. Maybe I was wrapped up in nostalgia, homesickness, or some naïveté, but I started thinking I was ready to return and do my part in helping Turkey succeed.

The skills I had acquired as a mechanical engineer could be put to good use in the country, hopefully helping to speed up its delayed technical development, if even in just some small way. Having seen how great the US had become through technological and social progress, I wanted Turkey to move forward in the same ways as well. This could be an opportunity for me to help Turkey develop its manufacturing industry and open it up to the rest of the world, building wealth not just for Nukhet and I, but for the Turkish people.

I was still working at Stevens, and I began to discuss this idea around the office. Most of my colleagues and friends, especially the Turkish ones, told me I was crazy.

"What would you go to Turkey for?" they asked. "You're making good money here, you're married, you have a life here, and you'll be starting a family soon."

All of this was true, including the last part—Nukhet was pregnant and we'd be welcoming our first child shortly. But I just kept thinking about Turkey and how the country had helped me in countless ways, making it possible for me to have everything I had, to accomplish my goals that led to my success as a husband, an engineer, an immigrant, a person, and a soon-to-be father. I felt that if I didn't help the country in return, I'd regret it forever.

Maybe that was childish, idealistic thinking, but I spoke to Nukhet about it often, and we made the decision together to return to Turkey. Without her support, I'm not sure what I would have done. She understood that we were potentially giving up a lot for me to follow another dream of mine. On returning to Turkey, I would have to do a mandatory two years of military service, and even though I was a mechanical engineer, I wasn't guaranteed to find work. But she believed in me and trusted me, and in so doing, I knew I couldn't—I wouldn't—let her down.

This type of shared life is integral to living happily and productively, but so many people are willing to overlook it for other accolades, such as money, social advancement, or fleeting relationships. Building a great life, succeeding in pursuits, and attaining goals are all for naught if there's no one to share that pride of accomplishment, that happiness, and that feeling of success with. When I was alone for those six months, waiting for Nukhet to arrive, everything I did, I did in an effort to prepare our home, prepare our life. Though it was good to make money and to stand on my own two feet, I found that with all of my life's successes, it was much better to have someone standing beside me throughout.

My daughter, Sedef, was born on August 10, 1966 at Jersey City Medical Center, and twenty-eight days later, we were on our way, my new growing family and I, to Istanbul. I knew I'd struggle, but I was prepared. I'd done it before and, most importantly, now I had Nukhet and Sedef by my side.

5

An Officer and an Entrepreneur

NUKHET, SEDEF, AND I LANDED in Turkey in September of 1966 with $17,000 in savings. It was a strange feeling, returning to the country in which I had been born and leaving the US behind. My gratitude to Turkey ran deep, but so did my love of, and gratefulness to, America, the people I'd met there, and my experiences over those past five years. My colleagues' sentiments rang in my head during the flight, those who had tried to convince me to stay insulated in the cushy life I'd created for myself in the US, but I pushed their reproaches aside. I was set in my plan, determined to help Turkey modernize and prosper in any way I could. There were just two main issues impeding my efforts: first, required military service. Second, I would come to realize that when it came to Turkish industry and manufacturing, I was pretty much clueless.

Turkey still maintains a conscription program today, a compulsory military service for all male citizens from the ages of twenty through forty-one. Though some are allowed to pay for exemption, that was not the case in the '60s. Besides, just as I felt the need to help the country progress, I felt that it was my patriotic duty to serve. I had been able to delay my service due to college and then working abroad, but I knew I'd have to put in my time when I returned. Though the political landscape of Turkey in 1966 felt uneasy now and then, the country wasn't at war, and I hoped the army would provide me with a chance to begin putting the new skills I had acquired in the US to good use, as I would be joining as an engineer officer-in-training.

The program lasted two years, beginning with six months of training in a military school. When we arrived in Turkey, my father-in-law picked up Nukhet and Sedef. While I was in training, they would be staying with him, my brother-in-law, and other family in my brother-in-law's apartment in Istanbul. It was difficult being away from them for half a year, but the base I was stationed at wasn't far, so I found as many excuses as I could to go visit them, mostly on weekends and holidays. Of course Nukhet's parents loved spending so much time with her and Sedef, and they were a great help to them while I was away.

Aside from missing my family, I didn't mind those six months. I understood that this was a necessary part of returning to live in Turkey, and I also thought the training could do me some good. Classes were held every morning, starting with lessons on the Turkish army's history, which I found fascinating, being a bit of a history buff myself. We then discussed all sorts of rules and regulations, our duties as officers, and what would happen in any war-time situation. The afternoons were reserved for running drills and exercises or for rifle practice and arms' training. If a war were to break out, we would be prepared.

The other trainees I met came from a wide variety of backgrounds. Many, like me, had attended universities and held professional jobs, while others were younger, fresh out of college. Anyone who had gone to college joined the army as an officer-in-training, whereas those who had not joined as the rank-and-file privates. Some would go on to make their career in the military, but most finished the required service and went into the public or private sectors, started their own companies, or returned to the jobs they had held before conscription.

With such a diverse group came an array of opinions, and I relished the opportunity to discover how these people from all different walks of life felt about contemporary Turkey. I explained that though I'd kept up on what had been happening in the country, I had spent the past five years in the US. It seemed that everyone was intrigued, and maybe a little impressed, so I often talked about my experiences in America, including my education, the people I had met—"yes, *the* John F. Kennedy'"—and my day-to-day life. Of course I mentioned the Corvair as well. I couldn't help but speak of the US with the highest of regards, saying how welcoming and free the country was, how as an immigrant I was treated with the utmost respect, and how I'd grown to love it there.

"If you ever get the chance," I said, "do yourself a favor

and go there. You'll understand what I'm talking about. You will be amazed." It never occurred to me that some of the other officer trainees would read into my reverence for the US as a potential sign of betrayal.

One afternoon, the commander of the school called me into his office—this was not good news. Since day one, I thought that this guy was a little unstable, and I had tried to avoid him at all costs. Everyone was afraid of him, as he was constantly barking orders and screaming at us at the top of his lungs, his face turning beet red, almost purple, the veins sticking out on his neck and forehead. He had a type of stamina in the way he insulted us and bossed us around that, if it hadn't scared us senseless, I would have respected.

So even though I didn't have an inkling as to why he would want to see me, I worried that I was in some type of trouble. As far as I could tell, I was performing just as well as everyone else there, better than some, and I wracked my brain wondering why I'd been singled out of the group and "invited" to his office.

I entered the room and he told me to sit in a chair across from him at his large wooden desk. "I want to talk to you," he said.

I was so nervous about what he was going to say next, all I could manage to squeeze out was a quiet, "Yes?"

"What did you do before you came here?" he asked. "Before training."

"I was living in the United States," I said, "getting my masters in mechanical engineering, and working at a place called the Davidson Laboratory at Stevens Institute of Technology, where I earned my degree."

"Interesting," he said. "Tell me more."

"What would you like to know?" I asked.

He responded with a litany of questions: "What kind of projects did you work on in this lab?" "How much money did you make?" "Did you own a house? A car?" "Do you have children and were they born there?" "Were you married here or in the states?" "Is your wife Turkish or American?" He was mining for all sorts of personal information, and I responded the best I could, as quickly as possible: I said we worked on all sorts of projects at Davidson, included some for which I needed US government clearance. I had made decent money, and told him how much. I explained that I had rented a nice apartment and owned a car while I lived there. I said that I was officially married in Turkey to my Turkish-born wife, and that we had our daughter just a few months earlier, right before moving back.

The commander looked at me with curiosity, as if carefully scrutinizing each answer. Then he said, "It sounds like you had a good life there in the United States, with your job, home, wife, daughter, *car*"—always with the cars—"so why'd you decide to come back here to our little part of the world?"

I began to explain my intentions, telling him that I had felt a calling to return to Turkey, to give back to this great country that had given me so much. I talked of Kilis, and the community and family that raised me, of the free education that had been crucial to my success, and of the country that I had so much hope for. I told him that I knew I could help Turkey continue to develop and move forward to be able to compete on an international stage and bring prosperity and stability to all of its citizens, no matter their social standing or religious beliefs. I was on a tear.

During my response, I saw the commander's expression begin to change, his typical tough-guy scowl softening uncharacteristically, his eyes welling up.

"Those bastards," he said, as I finished my reply.

"Excuse me?" I said.

"Those sons of bitches," he continued.

Not only was I confused, but I was at a loss for words.

"Do you know," he said, "that some of those other guys out there have been coming in here telling me they think you're a spy for the United States of America? The FBI or the CIA?"

Though I could tell he was emotional, I couldn't help but crack a smile, the thought of me being a spy so incredibly ridiculous.

"You left everything you had there to come back to Turkey out of a sense of duty, patriotism, respect—and these guys start spreading these vile rumors."

"None of them said anything to me," I replied.

"Listen here," he said. "If you have any problems with any of them, or anyone else, you just let me know and I'll handle it. You keep up the good work."

From that day forward, I didn't have any trouble. Service wasn't easy, but the commander was always in my corner, and that made my life a whole lot more manageable. The rumors apparently abated as well.

After those six months, all of the trainees in my program were awarded the rank of officer and then sent throughout Turkey to work on a variety of projects. I had wanted to live in Ankara to be close to some friends and family, including Ismail Agabey, my older cousin who had treated me like a son while I was growing up in Kilis. He had moved to Ankara years earlier. Luckily, a friend of mine's relative was involved in picking where all the new officers would be sent, so a good word was put in on my behalf. The next thing I knew, I was renting an apartment in a neighborhood on the outskirts of Ankara, reunited with Sedef and Nukhet, and living within walking distance of Ismail.

Over the next year and a half, I worked on two main assignments, starting with a stint at army headquarters in downtown Ankara. It was a government building, full of military offices, similar to the Pentagon in the US. I can't say, however, that I thought my skills were necessarily being used wisely in my first assignment.

Strangely enough, there was a small ginger ale manufacturing factory in the basement. Once the drink was bottled, it was given out to officers and workers throughout the building—I guess they drank a lot of ginger ale. I was put in charge of the facility, making sure that the machines were maintained and that no one at headquarters went thirsty. After six months, I was given a more prestigious assignment, joining a military engineering squad that was in charge of inspecting the

HVAC systems of any new army construction projects in the area.

I also taught HVAC courses at the Middle East Technical University. I really took to the position and worked closely with my students. By then, I had had plenty of schooling, and I believed I knew what made a good teacher. I especially pushed my students to understand the practical applications of what was taught in the classroom, and I regularly brought them on field trips to explain how actual HVAC systems worked. That all said, things started off a little rocky.

After the class handed in their first homework assignment, it was obvious that almost half of them had clumsily copied their answers off of one student. I gave them all zeros, and I told them that if they weren't there to learn, then they need not waste my time—I'd have no problem flunking them. I also told them that if they failed this course, they probably wouldn't graduate. This got their attention. They began doing their work—their own work—and we got along well for the rest of the semester.

When I came in on the last day of class, there was a bouquet of flowers waiting for me on my desk with a note that read, "To Sir, with Love," the name of a popular American movie. In the movie, starring Sidney Poitier, a new teacher faces resistance in the classroom, but in the end he conquers the class's hearts and becomes the students' favorite. I took this sign of appreciation as a compliment and thanked the class.

Since then, I have had the opportunity to run into a few of my former students. One of the more overzealous ones even stopped me in the street one day and tried kissing my hand. I didn't recognize him at first, which led to a bit of pandemonium. Once I realized who he was, we embraced and then talked for a while about the many things that had happened to both of us in the intervening years.

The only downside of teaching was that it turned out I wasn't supposed to be working outside of my military duties. I hadn't mentioned anything about the classes to my ranking officers until my service ended—they were not happy. Though I felt bad about that, I didn't regret my teaching experience, and overall everyone in the service was pleased with my engineering work, so they let it slide.

Though some are skeptical of conscription programs, my experience was a rewarding one, equipping me with skills that I would employ throughout the rest of my life. I was riding high on patriotic sentiment, attempting to repay my debts to Turkey any way possible, and I thought of my service as supporting my people, similar to how my community and family in Kilis helped each other, just on a larger scale. There's an intrinsic value in such actions, but more importantly, by getting involved it's possible to enact change.

I'm not saying everyone should go out and join the military—far from it—but there are plenty of things people can do to help support a program, community, city, or country that has made a positive impact on their lives. Military service was part of this for me, but I know it's not right for everyone, nor do I necessarily think this ongoing emphasis on military power makes for a healthy world anyhow. There are an endless number of organizations or institutions to get involved in, whether that's partaking in a community service, joining a grassroots organization, or going into local or national politics—heaven knows the US could use some young, forward-thinking voices in the halls of Congress today. Still another way is to start a business, providing jobs for a community and contributing to a better country overall, which is what I decided to do after my service ended.

My family and I moved from Ankara to Istanbul in September of 1968, where we rented a two-bedroom apartment in an up-and-coming section of the city called Etiler, which has since become a popular neighborhood. We liked the area so much that within a couple of years, we bought into a co-op in a new high-rise building, an apartment that we would stay in for almost a decade.

But in 1968, I was readjusting to life in Turkey. Nukhet and I were excited to be near our friends and family again, and we all spent a great deal of time together. We always had relatives willing to help out with Sedef, and Nukhet's and my relationship flourished. I therefore couldn't ask for more in regards to my home life. My professional life was a somewhat different story.

Though Turkey's manufacturing industry was falling behind many other countries', I was fortunate to have come back to Turkey when I did. The country was just then entering a small uptick in production capabilities, which I thought I could harness toward my goals. Though

I knew how manufacturing worked in the US, Turkish manufacturing was a whole new ballgame; luckily, it was one I could enter with little money or experience. My inexperience and ignorance could only be excused by my honest patriotism—I was convinced I would figure out a way to succeed both for me personally and my country collectively.

I decided that I would start a business that built production machinery. Not only would I need to hire people to build the machinery itself, but that machinery would then provide work for those who could use it to manufacture products. If all went well, this would be a start to dispelling Turkey's negative reputation in the industry. It seemed like a solid idea, even if it was a little light on details.

That year, I officially started my "production machines to order" business, *Enternasyonal Makina Sanayi*, or in English, International Machine Industries. Unfortunately, the work didn't just pour in. I began telling people about the business and my plans, and I always received the same response: "So what are you going to do?"

"Build machinery," I'd say.

"Yes, yes, I understand, but what machinery?"

"Manufacturing."

"Ok, but specifically?"

It was a valid question, to which I would reply, "Whatever—I'll build anything!"

The conversation would inevitably end with, "Well . . . good luck."

I didn't let anyone's negativity bring me down though. I understood that I was wading into murky waters, but I knew once I found my footing, the venture would take off. My entrepreneurial aspirations were strong, and sometimes that's all that is needed to take the first step in starting a new project, company, or business. Yes, I was flying by the seat of my pants, but I've always thought there's something to be said for winging it. Planning is important, but it can be overrated if the idea never moves on from the planning stage. I had an idea and I had the sketch of a plan—that was good enough for me to begin.

First thing's first, I decided: I sat down at my desk with a pencil and a pad of paper in hand, and I started brainstorming, writing down the names of all my former classmates in Turkey I had been friends with. I had kept in touch with a fair amount of them, so I pulled out my address book and looked some of them up. I called around, explaining that I was planning on building manufacturing machinery, and I basically asked if anyone knew where to start. I also got contact information for other people who could potentially be of help.

I didn't gain too much traction right away, but eventually one of my friends recommended that I contact a technician who he had gone to trade school with by the name of Necmi. Necmi had experience building machinery, and he ran his own small machine shop right there in Istanbul. He was currently looking for a partner to share the business 50/50, as his previous partner had recently passed away. Though I had wanted to go it alone, I hadn't had much success getting started yet, and it seemed somewhat serendipitous that Necmi needed a new partner.

I went to go speak with him, discuss my experience and my vision, and to check out his setup. Everything looked great, and we seemed to be on the same page as to our goals. He had a few projects lined up and was in desperate need of a mechanical engineer with my education and skills. I assured him that I was no stranger to hard work and that I was the man for the job. I'm not sure if it was my background, confidence, or enthusiasm, but he agreed, and we began working together.

Necmi had some good connections, and within that first year we built machines for a handful of clients. I was also able to get us connected with General Electric in Istanbul, where a close friend of mine worked. We produced a heat treatment furnace for GE, along with a number of conveyer belts. In the US, I hadn't had too much hands-on experience in building machinery, so this work gave me the opportunity to apply some of what I'd learned at school. Necmi had an excellent understanding of the business side of things, so he gave me a great deal of insight on running a machine shop in Turkey, and he taught me about what was going on in Turkish manufacturing and production.

Up until meeting Necmi, I had never been involved in fully operating a business from day to day. I knew very little about calculating the costs of labor, material, and overhead; handling payroll; managing employees; or dealing with distributors or other manufacturers. Necmi helped me understand all of these processes, as if I were attending my own private MBA class. After a little over a year, though, I thought that I'd learned all I could from him, and I was anxious to make my own mark.

He was a great partner, but I didn't think we were moving forward fast enough. While he was comfortable at the pace we were going, I was excited to push the envelope and make a bigger impact in the industry. I talked it over with him, and we decided it was best if we went our separate ways. He bought back my share of the business, and it was an amicable parting, with no hard feelings. We continued to stay in touch, share advice, and work together when possible.

That's when my true solo entrepreneurship endeavors as Enternasyonal Makina Sanayi began—I was on my own, ready for whatever might be thrown my way. I invested most of my savings into the new business, setting up a small shop with an office right above it in the center of Istanbul. The problem was, without my partner, I wasn't having much luck finding new clients. The GE work had dried up, or they had continued to work with Necmi, while I was left to seek out new potential opportunities.

I went back to contacting friends and former classmates, asking if they knew of any companies that might be in the market for some custom manufacturing machinery. While reaching out to people left and right, word got around that I had moved back to Turkey and had started my own business. It turned out that many of the guys I had gone to college with at the Technical

University of Istanbul had a similar idea, and they too were starting manufacturing companies.

A couple of old friends of mine, Necat Tasdelen and Omer Izgi, came to visit me at my office one day to hear about what I was doing, or trying to do anyhow. There were three rooms in the office, one larger than the other two. I had somewhat frivolously bought an impressive looking, big white desk, a nice chair, and some sturdy filing cabinets, which I placed in the largest room. The other rooms remained empty. When Necat and Omer arrived, we sat around my desk, first talking about my situation, then discussing what they were currently up to.

Both of them were full of complaints about their jobs. They'd been with the same companies since we had graduated together eight years earlier. They had issues with their bosses, their hours, the lack of progress they were making in their careers. They were, however, intrigued by my plan, though it was somewhat half-baked. Right then and there I had an idea.

"Well," I said, "if neither of you are happy, why not try to go into business on your own like me? Look, there are two empty rooms here—if you quit your jobs and start your own companies, you can work out of them."

They both looked at me like I'd lost it, but after going home and thinking it over—and me telling them I wouldn't charge them to use the office space—they each called me separately and said they were in.

Starting our businesses was not easy, but having friends nearby who were going through the same issues gave us the chance to commiserate together, swap ideas, and consider problems and solutions in a whole new light. The three of us, though not working together directly, were like one small community of entrepreneurs, not totally sure what we were doing, but doing it nonetheless. It made the daily anxieties easier to handle, the failures less devastating, and in the end, it all paid off.

After networking to my wit's end, at the beginning of 1970, I finally landed a lead. I had reached out to my close friend Arikan the previous year and told him to keep me in mind if he heard of any companies looking for machinery. Arikan and I had met in college in Turkey, and he had gone on to become a highly respected mechanical engineer at Alarko, one of the premiere construction companies in Turkey. A little while had passed since I'd last heard from him, but he called me up one day with some potentially good news.

"Dogan," he said. "You know what? There's this glass manufacturing company here in Istanbul—Pasabahce Cam—that's expanding, and I bet you they're going to need a lot of new machinery. Want to talk to them? I can introduce you."

I of course jumped at the opportunity, and he filled me in on the details.

Pasabahce Cam's original glass manufacturing facility was built in the 1930s or '40s, producing glassware for home and commercial use, such as drinking glasses and pitchers. By 1970, the company was ready to renovate their building and expand their offerings and operations. Alarko was working with them to help construct an addition to the existing facility, creating a warehouse double the size of the current one, and Arikan was in charge of the project. He got me up to speed about the company and what they'd likely be looking for, but he said he couldn't promise anything. I told him that was fine; I was convinced an introduction was all I needed.

The following week, I went to the site, where I met with the president of Pasabahce Cam. He greeted me when I arrived, and I think he could sense my eagerness. I told him all about my engineering background, my education in the US, the recent machines I had built with my former partner for GE and elsewhere, and I flat out said that no matter what kind of machine he wanted made, I was his guy. The president snickered a bit at my last statement and said, "Come with me."

I followed him into the existing warehouse, which was full of a kinetic energy, workers busily employed among all sorts of gadgets, machine parts, tools, and construction materials. He led me to a piece of machinery that I'd never seen. It looked like a large trough, with one end open, attached to a cast iron block. Inside the block were magnetic coils and flat springs.

"You can build any machinery, huh? How about one of these?"

"What is it?" I asked sheepishly.

He laughed. "An electromagnetic vibrating feeder from Germany."

"Ah yes, of course," I said, leaning in for a closer look, trying not to give away the fact that, until that very moment, I'd never seen, let alone heard of, an "electromagnetic vibrating feeder."

I looked it over, inspecting the construction, checking how all of its parts connected and interacted with one another. As I would come to learn, an electromagnetic vibrating feeder is used in the creation of glass as an intermediary step between the raw materials and the final product. There is a lot of loose material used in producing glass, such as silicone and potassium, that must be handled carefully. These materials are placed separately into silos before they are sent through the feeders. As they go through the feeders, the feeders' vibration is adjusted to regulate the amount of material that will then be fed onto conveyor belts or into specific receptacles before moving to the next state. Sounds simple, right?

"So," the president continued, "what do you think?"

"Well," I said, hoping he didn't notice the sweat forming on my brow, "no problem. When do you need it by?"

"Not so fast," he said, a devilish grin forming on his face. "We need forty-five of them. And we need them in three months."

I gulped, then said, "That's not an issue at all. I'll have a quote for you first thing tomorrow morning."

He shook my hand and sent me on my way, saying he looked forward to hearing from me. I decided not to mention that I didn't have a clue how to build one of these things, let alone forty-five of them.

I went straight to my office and locked myself in my room. Thinking over the project, I felt like I might start hyperventilating. At that point, there was no turning back: if the company accepted my offer, I would clinch my first deal, and my business would be up and running, on its way.

I went by the site the next morning and gave the president the quote, which he gladly accepted. He wrote me a check for 50 percent of the total payment—the other 50 percent would be paid on delivery—and I left with a sample machine in the trunk of my car. I'd have to take the sample apart, figure out how in the hell it worked, and reproduce the same thing forty-five times. Without that first payment, there was no way I would have been able to afford building a prototype, so that signed piece of paper in my pocket felt like pure gold.

Though I'd always had an entrepreneurial attitude, it blossomed at this time. I wanted to start nothing short of a Turkish manufacturing revolution, and I believed the way to do so was from the ground up. Turkey needed new, young, educated insights—the world always does— and I aimed to help provide them. That's one of the beauties of starting a business: innovation is necessary to a small business's survival, but the smaller it is the more flexibility it has, and the more chances it can take. Yes, I certainly spent days holed up in my office second-guessing my decision to move back to Turkey and open up my own shop, and it wasn't without its frustrations, but after I landed the contract with Pasabahce Cam, I felt unstoppable.

The US has developed a culture that applauds and encourages entrepreneurial efforts and small businesses, and I see no reason why this culture shouldn't be taken advantage of in America and in similar countries abroad. Starting my own business was the most gratifying aspect of my career throughout my long working life. The process taught me self-reliance in a whole new way. Every success, and every failure, was up to me, based on my thoughts and intuitions, decisions, and actions. I had the freedom to journey down any rabbit hole I wanted, and if I found a dead end, I'd just turn around and find another option to pursue.

I also wasn't ever truly alone, as I had the support, if only moral, from family and friends, including Necat and Omer. None of us really knew what we were doing, but we somehow figured it out. Both of them went on to start their own successful businesses: Necat produced pallet jacks that are used to this day throughout warehouses in Turkey, and Omer developed shipping containers and tanks to transport liquid materials from around the globe, which he distributes in Turkey. They both created good lives for themselves and their families, and we remained friends for many years—all beautiful things. Though we used to get together every time I visited Istanbul, and I still see Omer, Necat unfortunately passed away in 2018, but he left behind a lasting legacy that he would be proud of.

Many others from the Technical University of Istanbul's mechanical engineering department went on to establish their own companies as well, including probably 30 percent of my class. In some ways this growth in entrepreneurship developed from a lack of industry in Turkey, but it was also due to an entrepreneurial mindset that seemed to run rampant among the people I knew then. I think this may have also been a result of our backgrounds.

Coming from mostly lower- and middle-income families, we had always relied on ourselves, our own creativity and imagination, and it only seemed natural for us to pursue our own businesses in our professional careers. This growing entrepreneurial manufacturing community in Turkey held so many possibilities, and being at the forefront was truly magical. There was difficult work ahead, with new designs, new glitches, and potential problems at every turn, but I was ready to meet the task and the challenges.

When I got back to my workshop from Pasabahce Cam, I set the feeder down and started to tinker with it. "Forty-five of these, huh?" I thought to myself as I began taking it apart. "How hard can it be?"

6

A Revolution Approaches

I GOT HOME THAT NIGHT and shared the good news with Nukhet: I was officially in business. I told her all about Pasabahce Cam and the electromagnetic vibrating feeders they'd hired me to build. Since even I hadn't been familiar with these feeders, I wasn't surprised that she had no idea what I was talking about, but she was ecstatic just the same. She had believed in my starry-eyed venture from the beginning, and I'd proven that I would always be able to provide for her and Sedef, our family. It was a moment of incredible gratification, and I looked forward to getting started the following morning.

I was hoping that as soon as I opened up the machine and got a decent understanding of how it worked, everything else would fall into place, but I realized I couldn't do it all alone. My shop wasn't yet equipped with the tools and space I would need to create the feeders, so I asked Necmi if I could work out of his. Without hesitation, he told me he'd be happy to have me—was I ever glad that I had left our partnership on good terms.

After taking apart the sample feeder, I separated and cataloged each piece—every nut, bolt spring, and screw—but I needed a good draftsman to draw up depictions of the components, along with schematics of how they all connected. I decided to contact Pasabahce Cam to ask if they knew anyone. I was put in touch with a man named Sureyya, who was the head of the technical engineering department at the company's headquarters. Sureyya had heard about me, and he was glad I had reached out to him to ask about a draftsman. He sent someone over that afternoon who skillfully produced technical drawings for every single part. Sureyya also asked that I keep him in the loop on my progress.

Over the next three months, I spent every waking hour working on, or thinking about, the vibrating feeders. I was especially worried about the cast iron block that held all of the electrical wiring and circuitry. Not only was it detailed, but I knew that much of the materials necessary to create it could not easily be found in Turkey. If I were in the US, it wouldn't be a problem, since everything I needed could simply be purchased there off the shelves. In Turkey, I would have to scour the country for potential parts while also building pieces from scratch. Getting parts from the US was nearly impossible, especially within three months, but I could potentially get some materials from Europe.

In the end, though, I was able to hobble everything together and begin building the feeders. I also attended a trade show in Germany where I picked up a brochure from a company who produced the same machines.

The brochure detailed aspects of the feeders that I would have never thought of, and it also listed out the dimensions of every piece. This was a great help, as I compared the brochure's drawings to my schematics and adjusting accordingly. In the meantime, Sureyya was checking in on my work as I began making headway. He was incredibly supportive, as was Necmi, both of them encouraging me throughout those months.

But it was a grueling process, involving all sorts of aspects I hadn't anticipated. When I had first gone over the sample, the guts and inner workings seemed involved, but I felt that they couldn't be that hard to recreate. As I got into the project, I found that this was far from the truth. Eventually, I figured everything out, and the delivery day was fast approaching. I had Necat and Omer come by from our shop to take a look at what I was working on and get their thoughts. Sureyya and Necmi gave their two cents as well, and I thought with a last few adjustments, I was ready.

I owned an Anadol then, the first Turkish-made car. It was a tiny little thing with a fiberglass body, and my friends loved to joke around about it and give me grief, but, hey, it worked. It really was pretty dinky, though, and it could barely fit one or two of the feeders, let alone forty-five, so I had to rent a truck to bring them over to Pasabahce Cam's warehouse.

I drove there with butterflies in my stomach, feeling that I had more than just my fledgling business riding on this project. Many Turkish people in the manufacturing industry seemed to trust the Europeans' and Americans' ability to produce quality machinery, but they didn't trust their own countrymen's. Though Turkey had made some strides in the production area, locally made machinery was still looked down upon and had a reputation for being unreliable. With Enternasyonal Makina Sanayi, I wanted to disprove this fallacy, and getting these feeders just right was my first step in doing so.

At the warehouse, workers helped me pull out the machines from the back of the truck. Sureyya was there, along with some of the company's other team members, including a few staff engineers. As I set up the feeders, everyone crowded around, and I could feel my heart starting to pound faster and harder, banging so loud that in my mind I wouldn't have been surprised if they could hear it. I looked the machines over once more, then plugged them all in. It was the moment of truth. I took a deep breath and started turning them on, thinking that with this humble beginning, Turkey's time as a production powerhouse had come, and I would help usher in a new era of Turkish manufacturing supremacy. We all waited in anticipation.

Now, one of the most important parts about an electromagnetic vibrating feeder is that it *vibrates*, it says it right there in its name. Another imperative part is that it vibrates at the right speed, which is a fairly quick pace. So it's easy to imagine my dismay when the machines started up, emanating a soft hum, moving at such a snail's pace that they might as well have been sitting still. They barely shook, gyrated, or quivered—they certainly weren't vibrating enough. Most everyone around me burst out laughing, and I looked on in horror.

"Well," said one of the engineers, "look at that. Who would have guessed it?" A few more laughs followed his sarcastic remark, and they all started cracking jokes about the feeders. I turned the machines off and began scrambling, trying to see if there were some loose connections or an obvious problem I had missed. The team began walking away as I insisted that I could fix them. "Just give me a few days," I said.

They all laughed again. Over his shoulder, the engineer said, "Good luck getting this garbage working in a few days. You know the boss is going to want a full refund, right?"

I thought I was ruined. Their laughs echoed in my mind, along with the phrase "full refund"—I had already spent most of the money I'd been given on these machines, these worthless pieces of crap. I started panicking and flipping the switches on and off, shaking a few of the feeders, hoping they would spring to life.

"Dogan," I heard someone say. I thought everyone had left, but I'd been obsessing over the machines so intensely that I hadn't noticed Sureyya had stayed behind. "Stop what you're doing," he said. "Load those things up, and then come with me."

Unplugging the feeders and slowly carting them back over and up into the truck, I felt like I could cry. I couldn't help but sulk, fearing what Sureyya was going to say to me. I thought I had let him down, which made me feel almost just as bad as the notion that I'd likely be bankrupt within the week. When I finished, Sureyya motioned for me to follow him to a quieter corner of the warehouse.

"Don't pay attention to those sons of bitches," he said. "They're a bunch of idiots, and they don't know what they're talking about."

I forced a slight smile and thanked him, but confided that I wasn't sure what to do. Step by step, I explained the process I'd followed to create the machines, and he agreed that it seemed sound. I also reiterated my desire to put Turkey on the map when it came to manufacturing, especially within the country itself, and how I saw it as my patriotic duty. He nodded and smiled, having heard this from me before—he also had similar aspirations. During the time I had gotten to know Sureyya, I had found that he was an honest, intelligent man, a top-notch mechanical engineer who had been educated in Germany, and a devout Muslim who loved his country. I knew he wanted me to succeed.

"Dogan," he said, "I've been following your work these past few months, and I've seen the amount of time and effort you've put in. You're a good engineer, not to mention a good guy. I know you can do this, so it wouldn't be right just to give up now."

"I know," I told him, "but if this doesn't work out, I'm through."

"Trust me," he said. "I'm sure you'll solve this problem. Don't be discouraged. Just take the machinery to your shop and think about it: Where did you make the mistake? Most importantly, keep working."

I thought through my options. I could throw in the towel then and leave the warehouse defeated, personally, professionally, and financially. Or I could do what I'd always done: pull myself together, work my hardest, and come up with a solution to the problem. Though I was embarrassed by the failure of the feeders, I'd be much more embarrassed if I had to shutter my business, just when I finally felt like I was making some progress. Worse yet, I'd have to start all over again, figuring out how to make a living after having wasted all my time and money.

I thanked Sureyya and told him I'd be in touch as soon as I figured out a solution, then I walked out of the warehouse and got into the truck. On my way back to the shop, I repeated his words "keep working" again and again, almost like a mantra. I was in for a long night, and long days to follow, but I knew I could fix the feeders, I knew I could make them work—I had to.

It's surprising how seemingly small occurrences can have such colossal effects on one's life. That day was a major turning point, instrumental in my future success. Having Sureyya voice his support for me made me realize that I had attained some level of professional achievement that others could perceive. After all those years, I knew what I was doing, and even if the feeders hadn't functioned properly, someone else saw the value in my work and capabilities. All I had to do was double down and figure out where I had made a mistake.

I sat in the shop, staring at the useless feeders in front of me, asking myself why they weren't working.

Why weren't they vibrating up to speed? As an engineer, I have always approached such problems systematically, carefully checking my work, but when dealing with a complex issue, I like to take a step back to give myself time to breathe, clear my mind, and just think it all out. It's similar to entering a meditative state, erasing any other thoughts and oxygenating the brain to block out any surrounding static, focusing on the challenge at hand . . . And when that fails, it's best to reach out to people who know what they're doing.

Just like I had secured Pasabahce Cam as my first client by contacting pretty much everyone I knew, I thought about who might be able to help me with my feeder problem. Similar to how a community or family is important to one's personal life, a professional network is needed for a healthy professional life and career. This network should cover a large swath of experiences, including educational, job-oriented, and any other in between—who knows whose expertise or advice may need to be called on some day? To that end, it's good to maintain an up-to-date contact list, whether physically or digitally, that also includes relevant details about each individual, such as his or her job and position, place of work, and connections. I wish I had begun keeping such a database when I was a young man—instead I was left to rack my brains for hours, trying to think of who I knew who might have knowledge about vibrating feeders.

Finally, it came to me: Selim Palavan, an old professor of mine from the Technical University of Istanbul who had covered the concept of vibration in one of his lectures.

Professor Palavan had been adored by his students. Not only was he a top-notch teacher, but he was also a charming, funny guy. Having come from a country that is now part of present-day Russia, he spoke Turkish with a unique accent that all of us students joked with him about. He was good-natured, poking fun at himself as well, and in general he made his classes exciting and enjoyable. That said, if he'd been a jerk, I still would have contacted him—I would have approached *anyone* at that point if I thought they could give me even the slightest insight into these damn feeders.

I hadn't kept track of Professor Palavan since I was his student, but I looked him up and, sure enough, he was still at the Technical University of Istanbul. I checked his office hours and made an appointment for later in the week.

When I met with him, I told him all about the years since I had been in his class, my move to the US to study engineering, my wife and child, and my return to Turkey. He was happy to hear about my venture abroad, and maybe even more so about my decision to come back to Istanbul and take my chances in the Turkish manufacturing industry.

"We need more young men like you," he told me, "willing to stay here and improve the country, start a family, support Turkey."

I thanked him, but promptly moved the conversation toward the feeders. I explained how important they'd be to my business, if only I could get the first one working properly.

"Let me take a look at what you've got," he said.

I had brought along a sketch of the machine, and I walked him through each component, telling him the steps I had taken in disassembling then copying the Germany feeder. He listened carefully, occasionally furrowing his brow when considering a specific part of the diagram. It was hard to tell what he was thinking, but I barreled through my mini-presentation, figuring that the sooner I could get his input, the sooner I could get back to work.

"So," I concluded, "what do you think?"

He was silent for a while, staring at the sketch. I started growing nervous, worried that he had come across some fatal flaw that I had been blind to. It seemed like a lifetime until he spoke.

Then he looked up at me and asked just one question: "Well, did you measure the deflection of the springs?"

The words hit me like a ton of bricks, and I'm sure he saw my face turn as white as a sheet. Of all the testing and prodding I'd done, I had never tested the spring deflection, a rookie mistake. "Deflection" is a technical term for "travel," meaning how far a spring moves in length when compressed and extended, and how it moves up and down, or radially, during the process. If the deflection in my machines was different from the deflection in the original German feeder, then that could be the source of the problem.

After the shock of the professor's question wore off, I practically jumped in the air, then shook his hand and said, "Thank you, thank you, thank you," and rushed out of the room.

"Wait!" he shouted after me. "Hold on, there's more."

But it was too late—I was already out the door of the building, bounding down the front steps toward my car.

I immediately drove to the shop, cursing myself for not having thought of the deflection of the springs earlier. I inspected both the German feeder's springs and the springs on my machine, which I had copied exactly. There were six of them, almost one-quarter inch thick, four inches in width, and twelve inches long. What I hadn't considered was the heat treatment of the German feeder's springs. When those springs are made, they go through a process in which they are heated to a certain temperature and then cooled down at a certain rate— their deflection is affected depending on how hot they got and how quickly they cooled.

It was obvious to me then that the springs I used in my machines must have had a different heat treatment then the ones in the German machine. I therefore measured and compared the deflection between one of my springs and one of the German springs and found that they were off. Through some quick calculations, I discovered that if I added two more springs to my machines, they should make up for the difference in the deflection rates.

I attached two additional springs to one of the feeders and sat there, almost scared to turn it on, knowing that if this didn't work, I was back to the drawing board. Even if I did get it to function correctly, I'd spent so much money already, I'd need to ask for more to update all forty-five of them—but that was a problem for later. Holding my breath, I hesitantly flicked the switch. The machine came to life, vibrating at the right speed and screaming like crazy—I screamed along with it.

I shut it off, ran to the phone, and called Sureyya to tell him the good news. We talked it over for a while and I explained to him where I'd gone wrong.

"See," he said, "I told you you'd figure it out."

"Thank you, Sureyya," I said. "Thank you so much." I felt so indebted to his good will and support that I was nervous bringing up the next issue. "The only thing now," I continued, "is that I'm not sure how I'm going to be able to afford to fix all of them."

There was a pause for a moment, and I grew anxious listening to his silence on the other end of the line. "Well," he began, "why don't you bring the working feeder to the warehouse, show the team what it can do, and we can discuss from there?"

Second chances don't come often, and only a fool doesn't take advantage of them when they do. I hurried over to the warehouse the next day, set up my feeder, turned it on, and showed it to a number of the engineers. They all conceded that it was working correctly, and they even congratulated me. Then they gave me some signed paperwork and said I should go check in with Sureyya at the company's headquarters downtown.

When I arrived, Sureyya was happy to see me, but he may have been happier to see that the engineers had approved of the feeder. "Well done, Dogan," he said, "well done."

"Thank you, Sureyya," I said, "but as to the question of paying for all the modifications, I really don't know what to do. I don't have enough money to make these changes, and I know you can't pay me any more until I deliver the working machines. I'm just—"

Sureyya held up his hand, silencing me. "I'm not sure if you know this," he replied, "but the VP here also taught at the Technical University of Istanbul. His name is Serbulent Bingol—maybe you've heard of him?"

I'd not only heard of him, but I had actually had him as a professor one year. Sureyya suggested we go speak with him together, and he led me down the hall. When we got to Serbulent's office, Sureyya introduced me by saying, "You may remember Dogan. He was one of your students."

I stood there expectantly and said, "Hello Professor Bingol," hoping he would remember me. He looked at me quizzically, and I'm pretty sure he had no recollection of me at all, but he said, "Oh, yes. Dogan. How good to see you."

Sureyya explained the situation, praising my hard work and putting in a good word about my character and determination. Maybe it was his confidence, or maybe Serbulent felt bad about not remembering me, but whatever it may have been, Serbulent told us the money wasn't a problem. "How many more of these feeders can you update on your own, without any additional resources?" he asked.

"Four, maybe five," I told him.

"Ok then, how about this?" he replied. "Make the first

batch of five and take them to the warehouse. As long as the engineers sign off on them, we'll give you the second half of the payment in advance so you can complete the other forty. Sound good?"

To me, it sounded better than good; it was like sweet music to my ears. I was going to get paid, avoid bankruptcy, and be able to complete the project. I thought I was in business before, but now, at the end of 1970, I was truly legitimate. I completed the order, they tested and approved the machines, and from there my company took off.

Cashing in on my success with Pasabahce Cam, I designed a brochure for Enternasyonal Makina Sanayi, claiming that it was the largest Turkish manufacturer of vibrating machinery, which was true. I began sending out the brochure to companies I thought might be interested, and in no time at all I had to begin hiring staff to keep up with all of the orders I received.

One of the best lessons I learned from the growth of Enternasyonal Makina Sanayi was that success begets success—I was on a roll. In many ways, it's all about who knows who. If I hadn't reached out to everyone I could think of when I started the company, no one would have known it existed. I would have operated in a vacuum, and my business would have gone extinct. Instead, I worked both my personal and professional network, speaking with people I trusted about any potential opportunities—I can't stress this point enough.

Whether starting a business or simply looking for a job, hard work lies at the center of this effort, but building a network of people who can be relied upon is almost just as imperative. Without my friend Arikan suggesting I contact Pasabahce Cam, I may have never been aware that the company was growing and in need of the type of services I could offer. Without Professor Palavan or Serbulent, I would have fallen flat on my face, unlikely to get up again. And without Sureyya, with whom I quickly developed a bond, I wouldn't have had anyone in my corner when it counted the most, and I could have easily given into self-doubt and defeat.

Aside from Arikan, the majority of the people involved in my early business success weren't close friends of mine. As mentioned, people are willing to help when asked for advice or guidance. It's not that they just like to show off their expertise or knowledge either—though that can play a role—many simply want to be of assistance. There is something ingrained in the human condition, a sense of compassion or duty, that makes most people want to help others in need, or to give back if they've already experienced success. A strong network of such people is priceless.

The relationship goes two ways, of course, and in return for Sureyya's and Serbulent's support, I delivered the forty-five feeders they needed to expand their operations. Though I wish I could have done more for Professor Palavan, he was excited to watch his former student thrive, which, for him, held great value as well. Through teaching, he had molded many young minds, not knowing what would ever become of his students, so he was happy to count me as one who had become a success. And I'm happy to say that that success continued.

The Pasabahce Cam job, the brochure, and other early projects that came out of those, brought in a whole spate of new clients and business. We continued creating vibrating feeders and other related vibrating machinery for manufacturers throughout Turkey, but I branded the company as a "vibration and magnetic equipment manufacturer" once we began developing magnets as well—not the kind that people put on their refrigerators either. We started with magnetic conveyor belts and then moved into "electromagnetic lifting magnets," almost ten feet in diameter, that could pick up twenty tons of steel. Not to say any of this was easy—some days, producing all these machines in Turkey felt impossible.

For example, with the lifting magnets, we needed copper coils, which no one in Turkey made to specification. I had to beg and plead with a copper factory to convince them to fabricate some for us. Then I had to insulate the coil with fiberglass, dip it in a liquid silicon, and heat the whole thing to over 2,000 degrees Fahrenheit for about six or seven hours. There were no such furnaces in Turkey that we could use for this purpose, so we had to make one from scratch. In general, there was little to no existing machinery we could buy domestically. It could be a hassle, and some of the machinery we made came out looking like a Frankenstein monster, a hodgepodge of parts and pieces.

Katalog No: 55749

LM 30   Demir Kaldırma Magneti

EVF 350 Vibrasyonlu Besleyici

ESA-20   Elektro-manyetik bantlı Separatör

TEMSİLCİLİKLERİMİZ

MERRICK SCALE M F G. CO. U.S.A.
Otomatik bandtlı kantarlar
CARPCO, U.S.A.
Manyetik separatörler
ITIL ASSOCİATES INC. U.S.A.
Mühendislik hizmetleri
SALA İNTERNATİONAL, İSVEÇ
Konsantrasyon tesisleri

BF-600 Çanaklı Besleyici

KTS 50-B Kasnak Tanbur Separatör

İMALAT PROĞRAMIMIZ
1. Ağır Hizmet Vibrasyonlu Besleyiciler
2. Vibrasyonlu Konveyörler
3. Gıda, Kimya vesair Dozaj Vibrasyonlu Besleyicileri
4. Elektro-mekanik ve manyetik silo Vibratörleri
5. Beton Kalıp Vibratörleri
6. Elektro manyetik elle temizlemeli ve bantlı otomatik
7. Tanbur Separatörler   Separatörler
8. Kasnak Tanbur Separatörler
9' Kanal Separatörleri
10. Demir Kaldırma Magnetleri
11. Çanaklı Besleyiciler

TS 30/40 Tanbur Separatör

MSV-70 Elektro mekanik silo Vibratörü

makina sanayii a.ş.   **Merkez:** Gayrettepe TMT Han K.7 İstanbul Tel:66 06 85   **Fabrika:** Silahtar Sönnet Köp. Çamlık Sok. 41 İst. Tel: 21 50 60   Ank.BBr: Meşrutiyet Cad. 21/37 Tel: 25 35 90-18 44 18   Telex: 23458 Nal.Tr.   Telgraf: ENVIBRO

Production catalog showing Dogan's machineries, (1968 - 1978).

But one of my biggest points of pride was that we mostly used Turkish-made materials when building all of these machines from scratch. We would have solely used Turkish-made materials, but we weren't always able to find what we needed within the country. In the meantime, it was nearly impossible to import certain items from Europe or the US due to the weakness of Turkey's foreign exchange in the late '60s and throughout the '70s. Turkey was still going through a phase of constant government leadership turnover, with parties moving in and out of power, and very little was getting accomplished. Other countries saw this instability and took it as a sign not to trade with Turkey—I didn't blame them.

The materials that could be imported from abroad had to come through the Turkish government, but that was a slow moving process. It could take a year to a year-and-a-half after the payment had been made for materials to arrive in Turkey—by then, what was the point? We would have already lost the client or contract. So, though I'm not proud of it in retrospect, from time to time we had to take matters into our own hands and order what we needed in a roundabout way, which is another way of saying we had to smuggle materials into the country. It was a widely held practice, and in some cases it was the only way to keep our projects on schedule and our workers paid—by the mid-'70s, I had forty-six employees.

With so many clients and an expanding workshop, I moved the operation into a much bigger space, a fully functioning factory. I also started a new company, called

Tempa, which represented foreign companies from Europe and the US that were in related manufacturing fields. It was a way to help these companies make some inroads into Turkey, but also a way to help Turkish manufacturers connect with the outside world. I had the language skills, the education, and growing connections, and I knew I could help bring new products and materials to Turkey in time, while also introducing Europe and the US to the amazing work that Turkey was now producing.

I attended conferences abroad whenever I could, trying to understand how to increase our factory's output and quality and keep pace with other countries' manufacturing technologies. I voraciously read all of the trade magazines and stayed in touch with every contact I made. Tempa also gave me an excuse to regularly travel to Europe and the US to meet with the companies I represented.

By 1976, I was going to America so often that I actually bought a house in Port Washington, New York, on Long Island. My buddy Bob Madden—my friend who had taught me to drive many years ago, and with whom I almost got busted for not having a license to operate my $75 car—was the commander for the Merchant Marine Academy in Port Washington. I saw him often when I visited the US, and during one trip he told me about a house for sale near where he lived. I was no longer struggling financially, and I thought it would be a good investment and a nice place to stay when I was in the US. I looked at the house next time I was there and closed on it before I returned to Turkey.

Despite the bureaucracy of purchasing materials and the amount of work that went into figuring out how to build all these machines, my business in Istanbul was booming. I began to realize, however, that it couldn't go on like that forever, or, maybe more importantly, I couldn't go on like that forever.

In 1970, my son, Cenk, was born. As he and Sedef got older, I wanted to spend as much time with them as possible, but as the business got bigger, it was harder to be with my family, which I truly regretted. I had taken to putting in twelve-hour days, six days a week. I'd get up at 7:00 a.m. with just enough time to have breakfast with Nukhet and the kids, and I wouldn't return home until 7:00 p.m., just in time for dinner. Professionally, I'd never been more fulfilled. By 1978, the business was worth millions of Turkish lira and I felt that I had made an impact in Turkey. But in my personal life, I knew I was missing out.

I was getting worn down, and at first, I didn't want to admit it. Tireless effort had been so essential to my success, I felt like I'd be turning my back on my values, not to mention the company and my employees, if I tried to somehow slow things down, work less, or take a smaller active role in the organization. It just didn't seem possible, and even if it was, I couldn't decide if it was the right thing to do. The decision would end up being made for me.

In the mid- to late-1970s, Turkey began experiencing unprecedented political violence between right- and left-wing factions. The multi-party system that had emerged after the 1960 military coup had been wrought with problems since its inception, contributing to economic and social issues that had led to countrywide instability. In this climate, there had been an outpouring of political activism, both on the left and the right, starting with the students and then moving into the workers of the factories and beyond. Members of opposing organizations, including communists on one side and right-wing nationalists on the other, turned to attacking each other mercilessly in the open on the streets of Istanbul, Ankara, and other cities throughout the country. It was as if Turkey was in a state of civil war, its countrymen pitted against one another.

Though we had seen tenuous political and social situations in the country before, this new reality felt different. This was all taking place in the thick of the Cold War, and it was possible that Turkey could be torn apart, divided by Russia and the West. I tried to ignore the situation and stay the course at work, but it was harder than ever before. I was saddened by the state of the country, seeing it fall into such depths of despair, and I also started worrying about my family. What if they got caught in the crossfire of some skirmish? Or what if something happened to me and I was unable to provide for them anymore?

That's when I saw the writing on the wall—literally. I arrived at work one morning to the words "Boss your days are numbered" spray-painted on the side of the factory. I was stunned. I knew that many workers throughout the country had been organizing against management and large factory owners, spurred on by hardcore communists. With forty-six employees, though, we were only a mid-size operation, and I never thought I'd be singled out.

Early on in running the business, I learned that being friendly and understanding in such an environment pays off more than being stern and condescending, so I treated my employees well. I also felt a kinship with them, as many came from similar backgrounds as I had, and if my life had turned out slightly different, I may have been a worker at a similar factory as well. In addition, I was against the right-wing factions, who I believed were the instigators of much of the violence plaguing our country. Though I wasn't a communist by any means, I also didn't think of myself as a "capitalist," at least not in the terms that were used by the left to describe the rich factory owners who were known for exploiting their workers.

I had no way of knowing if the message had come from my own employees or some other group, but one thing was for sure: if whoever wrote it was trying to instill fear in me, they had succeeded. I began to think that they were right—my days were certainly feeling numbered there in Turkey, and I started considering closing up shop and returning to the US before something horrible happened.

Still, I was conflicted: I felt an allegiance to my country and to the men working in the factory. I had come to consider what I did for a living as noble, not just helping Turkey get its manufacturing industry up and running, but also creating work where there had previously been none. I provided steady jobs in a dismal employment market, helping people stay out of poverty and support their families. I decided the best thing to do was speak to one of my workers who seemed to have been riling up some of my employees lately. I hoped he could give me some insight into their mindsets. I also hoped he might be able to shed some light on the cryptic message that had been left for me. Though he wasn't an official leader of the group, they all listened to him and admired him, and I had always thought he and I were on good terms.

I had him meet me in my office, and I started the conversation by explaining that I supported the workers, but I didn't want to be forced into an ideological fight that could end up with me being killed. He scoffed.

"Look," I said to him, "here we have forty-six people, all from poor families. This is the only way they afford to feed their children. And you see my car? It's a piece of junk—I'm not some rich mogul. I come into work before you guys every day, and I leave after you. I thought this fight was supposed to be against huge corporations, not guys like me."

He looked at me with skepticism, and though I continued to explain my position, it didn't seem to sink in. To him, I was one of the "capitalist pigs" who couldn't be reasoned with, no matter my beliefs or treatment of my employees. I could tell I wasn't getting through to him, and when I asked about the graffiti, he ignored the question entirely. I then asked him how the workers were feeling with everything going on—he ignored that question too.

"If you want me gone," he said, "I'll leave, but only if you give me the severance I deserve—18,000 lira. Then you can do whatever the hell you want."

I was exasperated. "Fine," I said. I picked up the phone and, in front of him, I called our accountant and told him to give him the money. "Whatever he wants," I said.

I then told the worker to leave my business and me alone. With a pleased look on his face, he left my office, and I assumed that would be the last I'd hear of him.

Over the next couple of weeks, I kept thinking about moving to the US. I was hoping things would naturally calm down in Turkey, but the fighting continued, and everyone at work, and at home, seemed on edge. That year, my daughter Sedef had begun attending an English-speaking middle school on the other side of town from where we lived. Due to the distance, she had to take a taxi there every day, but the ride had started to become dangerous. Throughout the city, people were attacking taxis, hurling rocks and other objects at them. I started fearing for her daily trip to school, something that shouldn't be a commonplace concern for any parent—it was horrible.

Meanwhile, my accountant received a call from the MIT, Turkey's version of the CIA. They had a long list of questions about the factory and its workers, but they were most interested in the worker with whom I'd had the conversation in my office and who had left the company fifteen days earlier. "So you can confirm that he used to work for you?" the agent asked.

"Yes, yes," my accountant said, "but not anymore." He

told him about the message on the factory wall, pointing out that we didn't know who had written it, but that the worker quit right after it appeared.

"What about the money?" the agent asked.

"What money?" the accountant said.

"We arrested this very same man, and in his possession we found 50,000 Turkish lira, which he said he got from you—along with two guns."

Apparently, he had joined the ranks of one of the organizations that had been perpetrating violence across the country and was a suspect in a number of crimes that the MIT was investigating. The accountant explained that we had only given the man his rightful severance—18,000 lira—nothing more. The agent told the accountant we had been lucky—who knows what the man had planned? Maybe he could have come to the factory with his guns loaded, looking to dispose of me and take it over? When the accountant relayed the story, I knew then that I hadn't been needlessly panicking—this violence could have very easily landed at my front door.

That was the breaking point. I would never be able to forgive myself if something happened to my family in this pointless battle for power. That evening, I told Nukhet that I had made my decision: we were returning to America.

At first, she didn't want to leave, but I insisted that if we stayed, things might turn out bad for me—very bad. When I broke the news to my friends, they were all surprised. "But you're doing so great here," they said.

"You have everything you could want! It's going to be fine. Don't go."

"It's not enough to keep me here," I said. "If it was just me, it would be one thing, but I need to think about my family's safety."

People thought I was overreacting, but I'd had enough. Ironically, when I had left America to return to Turkey, everybody told me, "Why are you leaving America to go back to Turkey? You have a good job here. You're making money. Everything's good." Now that I planned to leave Turkey, people said the same thing about going back to America. But just as I knew to follow my heart and my gut when I had returned to Turkey, I knew to follow them again and go to the US. I sold the company as quickly as I could and got ready to leave the country.

I felt somewhat defeated, as if I was being forced out of my business and my home, but I was proud of what I had done in Turkey during those past twelve years. I had worked myself to the bone to achieve a dream, and that dream was beginning to become a reality. Though the revolution in Turkish industry I had hoped for had not entirely materialized yet, Turkish manufacturing was on the rise, and I felt that I had done as much as I could for my home country at that point. The factory I established employed nearly fifty people at a time, and we were producing all kinds of high-quality machinery, unlike any that had been made in Turkey before.

I'm proud of the men who worked for me, a number of who went on to start their own businesses, building and exporting machinery all over the world. Some run multi-million dollar factories, while others have smaller scale production facilities, and seeing them succeed on these various levels has been more fulfilling than I could have ever imagined. Today, manufacturing in Turkey is completely different. There are many large machinery manufacturers, and I like to think that without the factories of the '60s and '70s, like the one I started, the current manufacturing landscape in Turkey might not exist.

During those twelve years, Nukhet and I were also raising our children, though I have to give her all the credit. Without her, our kids would have never turned out so great. While I was putting in twelve-hour days, I always knew that they were being taken care of by the best possible mother, who was teaching them right from wrong and keeping them out of harm's reach.

Though I was disappointed by how things worked out with the factory, I felt that by trying my best, I had made a positive impact, which is sometimes all that can be hoped for. Hard work takes its toll, but it was in this work that I found happiness and success, helping Turkey, supporting my workers, providing for my family, and also reaping the financial rewards that come with endless effort. My return to the US would not be a glorious one, but I had no mixed feelings—I was ready to go back to my adopted home for good.

7

Return to the West

THIS TIME WHEN I FLEW into New York, once again arriving at JFK—the name having changed in 1963, honoring the late president—my life was vastly different than seventeen years earlier when I first came to America. I wasn't showing up with just a note in one pocket and a dollar in the other. I was now forty-one years old, with a wife and two children, had received degrees from both a Turkish college and an American college, spoke English fluently, and had run my own company for over a decade. I had become an established entrepreneur and business person, saved up some money, and started a family—by every measure, I was a success.

We settled into our new home in New Jersey, not far from my brother and his family. I no longer had to look over my shoulder every day in fear of getting stabbed or shot by a disgruntled worker, or becoming a casualty of a politically charged street fight. Nor did I miss the stifling air of Istanbul, where people were still using coal to heat their apartments; the pollution had gotten so thick that it had become hard to breathe in the city. Instead, when I walked out the front door of my house in East Brunswick,

I breathed in deeply and greeted my neighbors with a smile. Sedef and Cenk started school, and while Nukhet began setting up our new home, I set out to find a job. It seemed like my inclinations on moving to the US had been right, and I felt relieved knowing my family and I were safe and sound.

Still, something nagged at me. Now that I was in the US, I wondered if there was anything else I could have done to make the factory in Turkey work, to have grown it bigger and faster, and to have avoided the upheaval that led to my departure. I couldn't have stopped the social, political, or historical forces that had led to the current state of the country—I knew that of course—but I started becoming frustrated, thinking that for as much as I'd accomplished, I had also, in some ways, given up.

I talked to Ihsan about how I felt, and he told me to forget about it. He thought I had done the best I could, and there was no reason to wallow in the past, especially now that I was back in the US.

"Don't give it a second thought," he said. "You did what was right for you and your family, and all that matters now is what you do going forward."

I told myself he was right and tried to move on. I knew that once I started working again, I wouldn't be thinking about the factory any more. Who knew, maybe I'd achieve even more in the US than I had in Turkey? I had the talent, the drive, and the experience, all I needed now was a chance. I would come to realize that it wouldn't be as easy to find as I had expected.

Before I had left Turkey, I got in touch with one of

the companies in the US that I had been representing, a conveyer belt scale manufacturer based out of Passaic, New Jersey. Though I would no longer be representing them in Turkey, I thought that I might be able to work for their sales team in Jersey. It seemed like a good fit: I had helped them sell plenty of their scales to a major steel plant in Istanbul, I was familiar with their products and operation, and I'd be living close by. I had also become pretty good friends with a member of their management team. He told me there might be a place for me at the company once I moved to the US, and one of the owners agreed, so I assumed I was a shoo-in.

Unfortunately, my assumption was wrong. Once I landed stateside, I contacted the company and they said that, though they wished they could hire me, there wasn't a place for me. When I asked if anything might be opening up soon, they talked around the question and wished me the best of luck. It was my first dead end, though not my last.

For the next nine months, I set off on a fruitless job search. Unlike my professional network in Turkey, I only knew a few people in the US who could potentially help me. I began making calls to see what was out there. As it turned out, not much. I had one sales job opportunity come up at an auto parts store, but it was in a town in Pennsylvania that was a two-hour drive from my home each way. I decided the position would be more of a hassle than it would have been worth, as the pay was mediocre and I had never really been interested in working on the retail side of a business. I then started contacting old friends and colleagues from Stevens, former professors, and some people I knew from the University of Maryland, but I just couldn't catch a break.

I looked in the classifieds every day, and one morning it occurred to me that maybe I was going about this job search all wrong. That morning I saw a for sale ad for a small machine shop. I thought it over: Instead of going to work for someone else, why not start up my own business again? I had been my own boss for so long, returning to being an employee would probably have been a hard transition anyhow. I could feel my entrepreneurial senses tingling as I read about the small business and began thinking about how I could enlarge it and improve it. If I was able to do so from scratch in Turkey—with little money and almost zero resources—it seemed like doing so in the US would be even easier. I called the shop that day and spoke with the owner. It was a great conversation, and though he wanted more for the business than I could afford, I hung up the phone thinking I was onto something.

Over the next few weeks, I researched every machine shop and related company for sale that I could find in the area. They were all small, the perfect size for what I was looking for, and some of them sounded promising. The main obstacle I kept running into was that they were too expensive. I thought I might be able to strike a deal, but if the business was in prime shape, the owners wanted an astronomical price. Others, those that were just in decent shape, would have been cheaper, but most of the owners had planned to pass them onto their sons, or someone else in line to take over, so they would only entertain offers on the higher end. And any businesses that were within my price range were just in too poor of shape.

Simply put, I was stuck: I couldn't find a job, I couldn't afford to purchase or start a new business, and I was running out of money. Thinking that I'd be working soon enough when we got back to the states, we had bought a house and a car, and we were spending as if I already had a steady income, chiseling away at our savings without replacing it.

The same frustration I had felt over giving up my factory in Turkey came back to me ten-fold. I was constantly stressed out and full of anxiety, second-guessing my every decision. Maybe my friends and family in Turkey had been right; there I had been a success, in the US I felt like I was becoming a failure. Uncertain what to do, I was trapped in a cycle of self-pity and confusion. I became irritable at home, and now every day when I scoured the classifieds, I ended up feeling defeated, swearing at my misfortune.

I was letting myself get too caught up in my emotions, blind to what was going on around me. Failure is never easy, and having just come away from the factory, leaving behind what had been, up until then, my life's work, I only felt worse about my current situation. People throw out platitudes about failure all too often, telling others to gird their loins and get back to work. And though that's what everyone may want to do, it's not always possible right away—no type of empty slogan can convince someone to just get over it and move on.

I had to remind myself why I was doing all of this in the first place—for my family. If it were just Nukhet and I, we could have managed longer while I looked for a job; I could have even gone back to selling pots and pans. But as a father, I needed to provide, and I wanted to continue being a positive role model for Sedef and Cenk. I thought it was important for them to see that, no matter what, it's always possible to make one's way in this world. Spending time together at night when the kids got home from school and over the weekends re-energized me and helped me put things in perspective. I had reached other goals throughout my life that had seemed far-fetched, and I had overcome obstacles that felt insurmountable. I could do it again, and I had the best reason on my side.

I pulled myself out of my near depression and started to consider every possible option I had. If my engineering pursuits were a dead end, and I wasn't buying any type of machine shop, I needed to figure something else out—I would do anything I could. One crazy notion I had was opening a Turkish restaurant. Was I a good cook? Not really. Did I know anything about the restaurant industry? Not at all. So I'm not sure anymore why I thought this idea was a good one. Luckily for me, once I started doing some research, I realized how much was required, and I knew right then I would be getting into something that I would quickly want out of.

The next harebrained scheme I started brewing up was to import and sell high-quality Turkish rugs. I had toyed with this idea when I was still in Turkey, so I had purchased a few before I moved back to the US, thinking that maybe I could open a rug shop in Manhattan. I had mentioned the venture to my Uncle Ismael who told me I should speak with one of his friends who'd been in the business for nearly thirty years. The man asked me about my previous work experience and my profession, and when I told him I had been an engineer and ran a factory, he laughed. "I've been in this business since you were just a kid—trust me, it's not worth it. Stick with the engineering."

When I got to New Jersey, I sold all of the rugs within forty days, so I thought maybe I could make it work, but I decided to take my uncle's friend's advice and go another route. I figured if nothing else came together, I could try out the rug business again. But that's when a new opportunity presented itself, falling into my lap and changing the course of my entire career.

I hadn't ended up in East Brunswick by chance. I had decided to move there for a number of reasons. One was to be close to Ihsan and his family, but another was that an old friend of mine from Kilis was moving there as well, a man I had known since I was just a kid in middle school. He had left Kilis to attend a military academy in Istanbul and, years later, ended up going to Northwestern in Chicago.

I had lost contact with him over time, but bumped into him again in Turkey while I was running my factory in the '70s. He wanted to move his family to Istanbul and was actually looking for a job, but things didn't work out, so he returned to the US and settled in Alexandria, Virginia. He told me to look him up if I was ever in the area. My work at Tempa brought me to DC fairly regularly, so I reached out to him whenever I was there and we would get together.

After I moved back to America, he was getting ready to leave Alexandria and had been considering moving to New Jersey. At that time, I was staying with Bob Madden in Port Washington. I had sold the house we had there and was looking to buy a new one in the tri-state area. My friend and I met up in Manhattan and we talked over what I'd been seeing on the market. He had found an ad for a house in East Brunswick, New Jersey, close to the home of a Turkish doctor he knew, and asked if I would go look at it with him.

It was a great place along the Lawrence Brook, a small tributary of the Raritan River. There also happened to be a house for sale right next door. Though I hadn't been planning on buying a home that day, the next thing I knew both he and I were signing preliminary paperwork. Unfortunately, the house I was interested in didn't work out, but I thought the neighborhood was excellent, and I liked the idea of being close to old friends. I found a place nearby, and just like that, this old friend of mine and I were neighbors.

We talked often and invited each other's families over for backyard barbecues and dinners. In the meantime, more Turkish families were moving into the area, many within walking distance—some of whom we knew, some we did not—and a small Turkish community began developing. It was like the best of both worlds for me, Turkey and the US joined together in this little enclave. Still, not having a job was wearing thin.

I often spoke to my friends and neighbors about the troubles I'd been facing in finding a job or new business opportunity. One day, one of them suggested that I consider going into real estate. According to him, it didn't require a great deal of money up front, I could work for myself and be my own boss, and it was potentially lucrative. Still, I didn't know much about the industry, so I wasn't that comfortable with the prospect. Sure, I had bought and sold the house in Port Washington and bought the new one in New Jersey, but that was the extent of my experience. When I first moved back to America, I hadn't even known that I could apply for a mortgage.

So when I started looking into the idea, I was skeptical. Then, out of the blue, someone I knew mentioned that he had heard about an office building for sale. "It's a great opportunity," he said. "Apparently, there's a beautiful 50,000 square-foot glass office building in Eatontown, about forty minutes from here. It's state of the art and just waiting there for someone to purchase and manage. I'm telling you, it's a great price, and you could make a lot of money renting the spaces out."

For ten years, the building had been on the market, which seemed like an awfully long time to me. The previous owner had gone belly up, so the bank owned the building. None of these details sounded good, but the person who suggested I look into it blew off my concerns.

"That's better for you," he said. "The bank is itching to get rid of it."

Eatontown Executive Center, purchased in 1979.

He certainly seemed to know what he was talking about, though I wondered why he wasn't jumping at the opportunity himself. After thinking it over, though, I decided it was worth considering, regardless of my experience or lack thereof. I went to look at the building, and based on everything the realtor told me, it seemed like a sound investment, so I was leaning toward saying yes. It was more expensive than I had hoped, but I started to think that maybe this was a sure thing. Maybe this was exactly what I needed to get out of my slump and strike it rich.

Did that turn out to be true? In a word: no. But by then it was too late. I went along with my gut, took out a mortgage, and dove in head first. I probably should have spent more time thinking it through, but all I can say for myself is that I was excited, and this wasn't the first or last time my excitement got the best of me.

When I had started my manufacturing business in Turkey, I knew I could rely on my engineering skills, and I figured I'd learn how to run a factory, manage employees, and anything in between along the way. With this office building, however, I was entering entirely new territory.

Not all of the units in the building were being rented when I bought it, but I convinced myself that I'd have them filled up in no time. I began managing the day-to-day operations, slowly figuring out all the work that goes into running an office building. Only about 25 to 30 percent of the building was occupied, and only about $6,000 was coming in as gross revenue per month. This would have been fine if my expenses hadn't ranged anywhere between $12,000 and $15,000 a month. Between the mortgage, electricity, heat, water, cleaning, real estate tax, insurance, and repairs, the bills piled up fast. I also had to install sprinkler systems throughout the whole building.

It was all adding up so quickly, and I still hadn't been able to attract any new renters. I felt like I was sinking and that this whole plan was already a failure. I would walk around the building, lingering on two floors that were entirely empty. Both were simple, vacant, raw spaces, with no walls or partitions. I wasn't sure if I'd have to build these out, hire someone for the job, or if a company renting the floor would eat the costs. I wasn't sure about anything, except I was once again convinced I was finished. I asked myself how I could get new businesses in the building, and then, as I did whenever I hit a wall, I sought out advice.

One night, I attended a Rotary meeting in Eatontown. I had been a member of the Rotary Club in Istanbul for about four years before I moved to the US the second time. I had always enjoyed the organization's international focus and its stated purpose of bringing business and professional leaders together to do good for the local and international community. I also appreciated its non-political, non-sectarian approach, and its openness to people of all backgrounds, ethnicities, races, and religions. It was a very American organization in that sense, and when I came back to the US, I stayed an active member.

We had speakers every week who gave presentations on a number of topics, including ones on starting and running a business, which came in handy. While in the US, after being a member for a number of years, I had the opportunity to give a few talks of my own, and I went on trips to South Korea and Puerto Rico for Rotary International meetings. I always enjoyed the organization, not only meeting interesting people and new friends in Turkey, but in the US as well. My involvement also indirectly saved what would have been a short-lived real estate venture, but turned into a financial boon for the rest of my working life.

Most of the larger Rotary Club groups meet in restaurants or other function halls, as did the main one

I was a part of in Red Bank, New Jersey. But there was also a small Eatontown Rotary Club, consisting of about twenty members, that met at a bar on the same road as my office building, Route 35, and within walking distance. So one evening after work I decided to stop by. I went into the bar, looked around, and sat at the counter. An older gentleman next to me said hello and asked if I was there for the meeting. I told him yes—he was too—and we struck up a conversation.

"I like your accent," he said with a friendly tone. "Where are you from?"

I told him how I grew up in Turkey, came to school in the US, went back to Istanbul, and ended up here in New Jersey, living in East Brunswick but working in Eatontown.

"Oh, you work near here?" he asked. "Are you that Arab guy everyone's talking about who bought the empty office building?" He looked at me with a smile, and I don't think he meant to be rude, but I politely explained that, yes, I bought the building, but no, I'm not Arab but Turkish, two different ethnicities.

He apologized for his confusion and mistake, and introduced himself as the town assessor, a local government position tasked with estimating all of the property values in Eatontown. As we talked, it turned out that his wife worked at a real estate business outside of town on Route 35 as well. They had both grown up in Eatontown, and he seemed to know everything about the area. He was also eager to hear more about my plans for the building.

"So, how you going to rent that place out?" he asked. "It's been damn near empty for a while now."

I gave him a shrug and said, "Well, I think I just need to wait it out and eventually business will pick up."

I'll never forget the way he looked at me, shook his head, and said, in a matter of fact way, one word: "Bullshit."

I didn't know how to respond, but openly admitted that I wasn't too sure about what I was doing. I explained how someone had recommended I try this venture out, and I foolishly ended up putting all my eggs in one basket.

"I'm sorry, Dogan," he said, "but you're gonna have to do *something* to rent that place out—it's been empty for almost ten years. You crazy? What have you been doing over there this whole time?"

"I sit there every day from 8:00 to 6:00," I said.

"And?" he asked.

"That's about it."

He threw his hands in the air. "Okay, forget all that," he said. "This is what you're going to do: tomorrow morning, first thing, go buy a copy of the *Asbury Park Press*. It's the biggest paper around here. Check out the advertising section and create an ad to place in there. Just make it two or three lines, and once you have it in there, don't ever take it out, you hear me? Even if you have 100 percent occupancy."

"Well," I said, "I don't think I'll have to worry about that any time soon."

He laughed. "Trust me, this will work."

I figured it couldn't hurt, so I picked up a copy of

the paper the next day and decided to place an ad. In a moment of marketing inspiration, I also thought it might be good if I gave the building a professional sounding name, instead of simply calling it by the address. I came up with the "Eatontown Executive Center," which didn't really mean much of anything to me, but it certainly sounded official.

The next week, calls started coming in.

I worked around the clock so I could be available to anyone interested in renting a space, and I always attended to the needs of my tenants to make sure they were happy. Word started to spread that I ran a reasonably priced, well-maintained building, perfect for local businesses.

With the success of my initial marketing attempt for the building, I started brainstorming others. Not too long before then, someone had explained to me what it meant when something was called a "white elephant." The term refers to something that is big and expensive—such as a building, business, or project, for example—but has little value or utility. I was worried the Eatontown Executive Center would become a "white elephant," since it cost me a lot of money, but there was nothing I could do with it at first. As I started renting out more of the units, however, my concerns melted away.

My marketing idea was to flip the white elephant concept upside down, using a green elephant—green for US dollars—as a type of mascot. I went to a local print shop and had them print huge green elephants on large pieces of white paper, which I then placed in all the windows of the building that faced Route 35 so they could be seen by passing traffic. They may have looked a little silly, but they certainly got people talking. I started getting more calls, and passersby regularly stopped at the building, some just to ask what the elephants were all about, but many others to inquire about available space in the "green elephant building."

Dogan Uygur at his 'Eatontown Executive Center' office, 1990.

As things started picking up, I realized I could use some more help, both in running the building and in sharing the costs of doing so. I decided to offer up part of the business to my friend Orhan and my cousin Erol, who had moved from Turkey to the US in 1978 as well. They were both interested and bought a share of the building. It started looking like this venture might actually work out.

From there, I took it upon myself to learn every aspect of the commercial rental business. Though I had a knack for rushing into ventures without much planning, this time I simply needed to buckle down and do my homework. Every morning I came into the office at 7:30 and pored over all of the existing leases, spoke with the tenants, and tried to figure out the best way to make the building profitable. Though some days I ended up with crossed eyes and a headache inspecting all the minutiae, overall I enjoyed learning the business.

The effort paid off, as it became clear that the rents I was receiving from a number of tenants were way below the market rate. According to some of the leases, if new owners purchased the building, as I had, they had the right to raise the rents on a few specific spaces. I checked in with a lawyer to make sure I understood all the details, and then I informed those tenants that their rents would be going up. (This was also a good lesson in getting every deal in writing, which I've made sure to do ever since.)

I felt bad having to ask the tenants for more money, but without renting the spaces out at the market rate, there was no way I could keep the building open for long. I was also taking a risk: the tenants could easily say they weren't willing to pay the new rent and move out, which would be even worse for me. I went forward with the rent increase anyhow, and though no one was happy about it, most tenants agreed.

One tenant in specific was not pleased, and we ended up having to go to court over the matter. It was an unfortunate circumstance, but I explained my position in full and the judge ruled in my favor. Though my relationship with the tenant wasn't the best for a while after that, things eventually smoothed over.

Meanwhile, I had new businesses moving into the building, which meant I was constantly busy. Among them was a young tech company that was working with an early iteration of the Internet—I of course didn't know what that was, few people did then. The tech guys were rarely there, but would call me occasionally to ask if I could go into their office and press some buttons or flip some switches. Who knows what I was doing, but I liked helping. Only later did I understand what they had been working on in there among all of those screens, wires, and heavy-duty electronics.

I also managed to rent out one of those two floors that I had begun to consider cursed. The State of New Jersey took it over for one of their small governmental departments. They needed me to build up the space, so after they gave me the floor plan, I hired on a small crew to help out. Between a carpenter, plumber, electrician, and me, we had a whole team and did the majority of the work ourselves.

For twenty years I kept that ad in the paper, and for twenty years it worked. My old workaholic attitude returned, and I started putting in twelve-hour days, six days a week again, as I had when I was running the factory in Turkey. Cenk and Sedef were getting older, which meant college tuition, car payments, new hobbies—being a father certainly adds up. But it was all worth it. The Eatontown Executive Center paid for all of our expenses, for our life together, and I looked back on the slow start of my new career in the US as nothing but a blip in time.

The $6,000 per month gross income that the building generated when I bought it morphed into $60,000 per month gross income when I sold it in 1999. After all those years, my precarious real estate venture had become a prosperous one, and my instincts and taste for the business had grown exponentially. I took some of the money I earned from that sale and bought five strip mall shopping centers, entirely renovated three of them, and then turned around and sold the whole lot for twice as much as I had purchased them.

Real estate ended up serving me well. Not only did I continue to satisfy my entrepreneurial desires, be my own boss, and make a few bucks, but I also learned a whole range of new skills that I could use elsewhere in my life, skills that I had never much considered—it's always surprising the things people learn when they're forced by circumstance. One summer, for example, while Cenk was home from college, we started flipping houses together. The Eatontown Executive Center was going well, but I was always looking for ways to generate some extra income and Cenk needed a summer job.

For a while, I had been noticing the number of houses in foreclosure throughout New Jersey. I realized that if I could purchase a few of these homes at a low price, I could fix them up and sell them, not only making a small profit, but also helping whoever may be moving into them—some were nearly uninhabitable when I bought them. I'd been performing plenty of the work myself inside the Eatontown Executive Center, building partitions, putting up drywall, and other basic carpentry. I thought the small crew I'd hired to help me there would be willing to go in with me on this foreclosure business as well.

So I told Cenk, "Don't worry about getting a job. You're going to come work for me."

"Doing what?" he asked.

"Flipping houses," I said.

He looked perplexed. "But Dad," he said. "We don't know the first thing about flipping houses. Do you have any idea how this business works?"

I laughed and told him, "Well, that's never stopped me before."

He laughed along with me and agreed to help.

Together that summer we learned how to value houses, check mortgages, research the viability of a project, pull the titles from city hall, and figure out potential earnings. We set up a whole system and ended up buying three houses to start, all of which were vacant. Though there were some bumps in the road, we refurbished the homes, making sure they were great both inside and out, and we turned them around before Cenk returned to school that fall.

I made sure to explain to Cenk that success doesn't always come that easy. And that's truly what I learned from moving back to the US. No matter how much time and effort one spends on a business or a project, there will always be setbacks, there will always be failures. The only thing I could do in such a situation was pull myself up and get back to work, pressing forward harder and with more resolve than ever before. If I didn't put in all that I had, I wouldn't succeed, and even sometimes when I felt like I couldn't have done anything more, I still had to contend with failure. Things don't always work out, but there's always a way to make something else come together. There's always a workaround or a new direction to take, a plan to be hatched that will lead to achieving any long-term goal.

My real estate ventures were going so well that I began to expand. I continued buying and selling foreclosed houses, and within three years, I'd flipped around thirty of them. One of them ended up being a house that I held onto in Freehold, New Jersey, which Nukhet and I live in today, as we have for the past twenty-five years. In every renovation project, I used the same team of workers that I had put together to do repairs and construction at the Eatontown Executive Center. They were invaluable, not only in rehabbing these houses, but also in a few other projects I picked up. I bought another commercial building in Eatontown, this one a bit more manageable at two-stories and 4,000 square feet, along with a small four-unit building across from the Eatontown Executive Center. By then, I just couldn't help myself—the real estate bug had bitten me.

Walltownship Shopping Center, purchased and renovated in 2005.

As I got older, I had come to look forward to new challenges and the opportunity to continue learning. All of my new ventures have brought me joy, and I believe staying busy has certainly led to my longevity and happiness. For example, I started working with my cousin Teyfik in Istanbul, who ran a Turkish glassware company. He had been telling me about the popularity of his cut glassware used for tables and similar items. He wanted to sell them into the US market and asked me if there was any way I could lend a hand. As with many of my business prospects, I reasoned that what I didn't know—which was very little in this case as well—I could figure out, and I told him I'd be happy to look into it.

I went to a number of trade shows to get an understanding of the market and to learn how people actually went about selling these things. I developed a strategy and figured out some of the logistics before we set up a warehouse in Asbury Park. After a couple of years, Teyfik decided he wanted to focus on the Turkish market, so we shuttered the US operation, but I had appreciated the opportunity just the same. I also did two renovation projects with my team for AT&T in East Brunswick, New Jersey, and two small projects for the US military at their base in south Jersey. Without realizing it, I'd become something of a general contractor—I had my hands in a little bit of everything.

After twenty-six years in real estate management, I felt I had succeeded on my own terms and in a way that I could be proud of. I never cheated anyone or ripped anyone off; I always stuck to my word; and I provided services that people needed, that helped them run their businesses and take care of their families. Not a bad way to enter retirement—which I was certainly getting ready for, as was Nukhet.

Though I was busy throughout that time, working up to fourteen-hour days, Nukhet was always supportive, and, in turn, I supported her. After both our kids headed off to college, she decided to continue with her education, starting with night school at Parsons and then on to FIT in New York, where she took art classes. It was something she always wanted to return to, and I was so proud of her when she did. She had never lost her artistic talents— they only increased with age. Just as education has been important to me, it has been important to Nukhet as well, though she gave her time willingly earlier in our marriage to concentrate on raising our children.

When she finished at FIT, she started her own small business designing and manufacturing handmade home textiles, including napkins, tablecloths, and placemats, all with a Turkish design flare—the response was incredible. She opened a wholesale business in Eatontown at one of my buildings and a workshop in Istanbul. We had begun returning to Turkey often, as the situation there had stabilized and we wanted to continue seeing more of our friends and families as we all aged. This worked out well, as Nukhet could regularly check in on the pieces being produced in her workshop.

In addition to the space in Istanbul, Nukhet began an outreach effort in Turkey for lower-income women, mostly mothers, who she and her other employees taught how to make some of these pieces, especially those based off traditional Turkish design styles. These women had few employment opportunities, but they could create these textiles from home while they took care of their children or other family members. Nukhet paid them well, and the extra income could do wonders, helping many struggling families. She saw it as a way to give back, and she employed nearly two hundred women in this program.

Unlike me, Nukhet didn't have to combat the failures and financial close calls that I had to: it turned out she was not only a born designer, but a born businesswoman. Her textiles went on to win a first place design award in a home textile show in New York, giving her exposure that has led to her products being sold all over the country, from the east coast to the west, and the world, from Japan to England.

Her napkins have been used to entertain the British royal family here in the US; have appeared on the tables of Hollywood celebrities, including John Travolta and Sofia Vergara; and have even been set in the White House. I don't mean to boast, I'm just so very proud of my wife's great accomplishments.

When she told me about her work being featured in the White House, I playfully asked if I had ever relayed the story about how I had met President John F. Kennedy in the Rose Garden.

"Yes," she laughed. "I think I've heard that one before." And with that, she leaned in and gave me a kiss.

8

A Man of the World

I'VE ALWAYS BEEN ONE TO keep busy, no matter the circumstances, so when I retired I saw no reason to simply kick up my feet and sit around the house. After I sold the strip malls, I took advantage of a type of freedom and flexibility that can only come with age, one that has been essential to staying fulfilled and content as I've gotten older. There's always more to do, more to accomplish, and more to see, learn, and experience.

Even when I "retired," I wasn't totally out of the real estate game, holding on to one piece of property that I continued managing until I sold it in 2017. Nukhet ran her business until that year as well. I'll admit, though, that when I got rid of that final building it was a relief. Both Nukhet and I felt so fortunate about how our lives had turned out, and we were happy to focus our attention on the many other things aside from work that brought us joy. We looked forward to travelling, returning to old hobbies, and visiting with our friends and family.

When we were young, we thought Miami was an exotic destination, but as we got older we were lucky enough to be able to visit places all over the world; ones that I could barely begin to imagine when I was young, from Europe to Asia, South America to the Caribbean, and all over the Middle East and the US.

Every place had an impact on me: experiencing the serenity and mass of Alaska's nature, swimming in the clear blue waters surrounding Bora Bora and Tahiti, falling in love with the architecture of Barcelona, walking up to and along the Great Wall of China, and peering out onto the great chasm of the Iguazu Falls that separates Argentina and Brazil. We walked the major cities of Europe—Paris, London, Munich, Amsterdam, Rome—and lost ourselves amidst the ruins of Athens.

We found the people of South America to be some of the kindest, on our trips to Rio de Janeiro, Columbia, and Chile. We've been east to Russia, Prague, and Budapest, and further east to Malaysia, Indonesia, the Philippines, Japan, Thailand, South Korea, Hong Kong, and Bangkok. One of my fondest memories is of visiting Egypt and witnessing the size and power of the pyramids first-hand. Though I had read articles about them and their construction and seen photos in *National Geographic* and other magazines and books, nothing could have prepared me for coming face to face with the Great Pyramid of Giza—it was mind-boggling. I hadn't truly comprehended how impressive it was until I was standing there, marveling at how the Egyptians had built this humongous structure thousands of years ago.

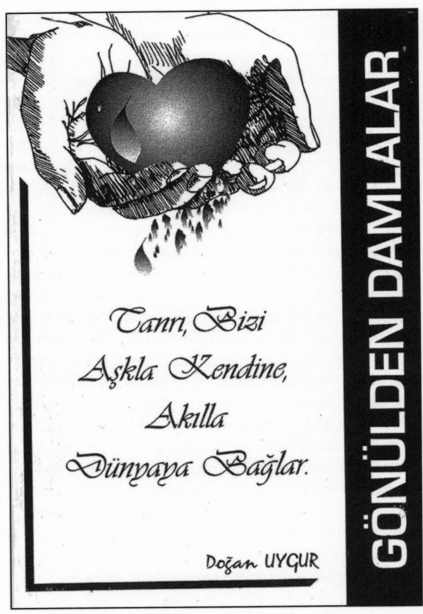

Tanrı, Bizi

Aşkla Kendine,

Akılla

Dünyaya Bağlar.

Doğan UYGUR

GÖNÜLDEN DAMLALAR

"Drops of my heart", a series of Turkish poems written by Dogan Uygur.
Cover designed by Dogan's brother-in-law.

I wish I had been able to go to all of these places when I was younger, but better late than never. When travelling, a transformational process occurs, not only through experiencing other cultures, but through moments of self-reflection, realizing that though we are individually just a small, tiny part of the world, collectively we make up humanity, tied together no matter where we are born, what we believe, or where we reside. I encourage everyone to go out and search for this experience. Don't break the bank of course, but saving a few bucks and making time to travel enriches life to no end. We are all global citizens today, and part of this responsibility is to embrace and understand the world around us, no matter how near or far.

In addition to travel, in retirement I have returned to the creative pursuits that I always enjoyed, poetry in particular. Since the mid-'60s, I had jotted down some lines and verses here and there, but after I retired, I was able to give more time to the craft in earnest, writing new poems and revising old ones. Poetry has given me an artistic outlet like the one I found in acting those many years ago. Though of course the meaning of each line is important, I love the musical element of poetry, the way the rhythm of the language comes to the ear, or how a witty rhyme plays out. When writing, I try to create a musicality, just like the Ottoman-era poets from generations ago, and I read every poem aloud, as I am a strong believer in the oral and auditory aspect of the art.

I went as far as to put together a small book of my poetry, in Turkish, titled *Gönülden Damlalar*, which translates to *Drops from My Heart*. The twenty-three poems range in subject, though they all mirror my life in some way, from my days living in Turkey to my life in the US. There are poems about my family—Nukhet and the children—my upbringing, and my social and political beliefs, but there are also observations of everyday life. For example, one of my favorites from the collection is called "Subway," based on my first experience riding in the New York City subway in the 1960s:

It approaches like a wild beast
People move like a flood in its wagons
These are arteries of New York
If they are clogged, the whole city will be paralyzed
Underground stations, dark and cool
Dangerous and scary, especially at night
In the subways: people, people, and more people
Parading like a movie clip
Yellow, black, red, white, skinny, tall, and large
Every race and color, running in a hurry

It may not be Whitman, or Yahya Kemal Beyatli, but I'm proud of how the book turned out. I printed about a hundred copies and gave them to Turkish friends and family. Many of them were surprised; most knew that I had a love of poetry, but few realized that I had been dabbling in writing it for many years. Maybe because of that alone, they were impressed. Regardless, everyone gave me positive feedback.

Then again, no matter what they had thought would have be fine by me. Writing poetry has given me joy and peace, just as any creative activity should—it's not about what others think but about what I think, how it makes me feel and how it gives me an opportunity to reflect over my life and the world around me.

It's always good to have some creative projects to keep the mind sharp, whether that's writing, playing an instrument, or producing any other kind of art. Though many people define themselves by their jobs—or are defined by others by their jobs—everyone is multi-faceted, and it's good to indulge these other parts of life, especially as one gets older.

Just as important as my creative endeavors, I've never given up on my educational ones. No one is too old to stop learning new things or to question and challenge long-held assumptions or beliefs, especially during times of political and social change, which I've lived through both in Turkey and in the US. Education was so significant in my young life, it's no surprise that it has remained so as I've grown older. I'm amazed—not to mention horrified—when I hear people my age, or younger, say that they've learned all they need to know, that their mind is made up and can't be changed at this point, so why bother? These are the same people who rarely read books or think outside of the box and, instead, tend to fall into the trap of the out-of-date adage that old dogs can't learn new tricks—trust me, we can.

Part of that continuing education for me has been both religious and political. For a number of years, I'd been moving further away from the Islamic faith, all religious faiths for that matter. Having grown up in the secular shadow of Ataturk's revolution, it may not be a surprise that later in my life I rejected Islam in full. Around when I turned fifty, I began to feel that religion in general wasn't for me, finding that much of what I was taught about religion when I was young—and much of what continues to be taught today—is inaccurate or simply untrue.

In 1990, I helped a Turkish-American community in Pennsylvania purchase and establish a mosque and educational center. The community had been growing in that area since the 1960s, when one young man moved there from a small village on the Black Sea coast of Turkey. Eventually, his friends and family arrived, putting down roots. They started an association that a friend of mine got involved in and he invited me to join. Though I had begun questioning my religious beliefs by then, it seemed like a worthy cause; the community was not all that affluent and the mosque would also act as more than just a place for religious services, doubling as a community and resources center where Turkish history and language would be taught.

When the mosque opened, we invited a well-known professor of Islamic theology from Turkey, Yasar Nuri Ozturk, to lead a group discussion on religion. I knew he was fairly progressive, and I looked forward to his talk, but I hadn't expected it to have such an impact on me. Throughout the conversation, he repeatedly told the audience to make sure that we truly read the Quran. That to have a deeper understanding of the book, we must know exactly what is actually written in it.

With my faith already faltering, I wasn't sure if it would be worthwhile to revisit the Quran and read it in its entirety. I thought I generally knew what it was all about, relying on what I had remembered from reading passages of the book in my youth. There was something about the way Ozturk insisted, however, that convinced me to give it another try. And in the spirit of continuing my education, I cracked the cover of an old Turkish copy I had lying around the house and began to read.

That's when I truly started re-examining my religious values and beliefs in a serious way. I decided to read the Old Testament and the New Testament, along with other books on the history of religion, including the excellent *The Bible Unearthed* by Neil Asher Silberman and Israel Finkelstein, which takes a more scientific approach to the Old Testament. I also read about the history of Islam, Judaism, and Christianity, all of which have roots in similar theological thought. This was a period of awakening for me.

On close inspection, all three of the main holy books felt more political and social than spiritual. I thought about the effect they'd had on history—the unbelievable number of people killed in the name of religion, the rise and fall of empires—and it occurred to me that for thousands of years people have followed what others have told them about these texts without actually ever reading them. For example, the Catholic Church didn't translate the New Testament from Latin to modern European languages until 1450, which had been a way to maintain power over the people, as the church's leaders could therefore claim that just about anything was written in the Bible.

Similarly with the Quran today, there are fifty-seven Muslim majority countries in the world, but only a handful of them are Arabic speaking, which is the primary language the Quran is presented in. Many Muslim leaders tell their followers that reading the Quran in any other language aside from Arabic is null and void, again in an attempt to preach the words as they interpret them, not necessarily how they are written. I took these facts into account as I tried to understand each religious book. In doing so, I considered them differently than I ever had before, almost as if they were textbooks, to better understand the actual ideas within them, not just what I'd been taught—and most people are taught—as children.

In studying them, I found it was as much about reading in between the lines as it was reading the verses themselves. I also found that they are chock full of concepts that do not apply to the modern world whatsoever; the Quran condemns donkeys, for example, which I find particularly humorous, since all I ever wanted as a boy was a donkey to get from one piece of our family's land to another. I came to the conclusion that all of these books must be handled with care and skepticism, and though I fault no one who finds solace in religion and religious teachings, I have developed a new understanding of them and have become agnostic. I would have never thought that I would begin to see Islam and religion in such a new light once I hit my fifties, but it only goes to show how people continue to develop throughout their lives.

Recent changes in Turkey have also contributed to my disillusionment with Islam. There has been a shift toward more fundamentalist Islamic thought throughout the country, propagated by the government. Today, Turkey is much more religious than during my childhood, relying on Islamic teachings in public school instead of what had previously been a secular curriculum. During the past fifteen years, the education system has been revamped, and in many regards destroyed, by the administration. Instead of promoting science-based, factual education, a more religious-based system has taken hold.

It's unbelievably destructive for the Turkish people, taking the only modern Muslim nation and moving it backward toward the hardline religiosity of places like Iran and Saudi Arabia. It leads me to believe that many people during Ataturk's revolution didn't truly understand what he had been saying, but only acted as "yes-men." If people had truly listened to Ataturk, they could have seen that he was serious about his belief in a secular country, one not ruled by blind religious thought.

Maybe my move away from faith is somewhat rare; I have seen many more people become closer to, rather than further away from, religion as they age. I would never tell people to disavow their faith, to give up on their beliefs simply because I've taken a different direction in my life, but I always urge others to inspect what they've been taught and take time for introspection and education.

It seems that many people who claim to be Christian, Jewish, Muslim, or any other religion, have never actually read their most basic religious texts in full, whether that's the Bible, the Torah, the Quran, or any other such material—if someone were to tell me that only 0.5 percent of the whole population have done so, I wouldn't be surprised. Though that's understandable—everyone lives a complicated, busy life—I also think it's important to give one's self the opportunity to continue learning and consider one's beliefs with an exacting eye, an open mind, and an open heart.

This idea doesn't just apply to religion either, but to politics and social thought as well. I've always been fairly liberal, but as I've gotten older, my progressive attitudes have grown. I don't see them as radical as much as I see them as commonsense.

Benjamin Disraeli, a conservative, two-term UK prime minister in the 1800s, famously said, "If you're not a liberal when you're twenty-five, you have no heart. If you're not a conservative by the time you're thirty-five, you have no brain." That has not been my experience. The longer I have lived, the greater empathy I have gained toward others, and the greater my appreciation has grown of the contribution of others to my success.

It is incomprehensible that in such a prosperous, forward-thinking country like the US, inequality persists, a fear of immigrants runs high, climate change is debated, the president wants to practice an outdated form of isolationism, and people can't afford healthcare—some can't afford food. Like Turkey's trajectory, America's is worrisome as well.

Living in the US today is in stark contrast to living in the country when I first came here, when immigrants were encouraged to move to the US, America was on the verge of positive social change, there were good, high-paying jobs for middle-class and working-class people, and opportunities were abundant if they were sought out. Unfortunately, America today reminds me of the Roman and Ottoman Empires. The Empires' hubris contributed heavily to their downfall, just as I fear the current US administration's hubris will lead to our downfall. Whether on Twitter, in front of the UN, or in his regular press appearances and speeches, when our president speaks about "greatness" while demeaning other countries, not to mention whole groups of people, he brings shame to all of us here in America.

And it's not just the US. This conservative streak is multiplying—whether in the Philippines or Brazil, Hungary or Poland, Russia or Turkey, and many places in between—as if certain groups of people want to stop the clock and return to the Middle Ages. This attitude, however, is a fight against nature. Now I may not be a scientist by any means—I'm just an old-school engineer—but even I know that ever since the big bang, the world has been in a constant state of evolution. Today, humans continue to progress physically, emotionally, technologically, socially, and mentally, so those who resist change are actually resisting the natural development of a free society.

I've seen progressives get blamed for so many ills when all they're trying to do is help others in need. Right-wing pundits and critics decry anyone pushing for progress as a "communist," as if a country supporting its people through affordable education and health care, living wages, and social safety nets is akin to North Korea. They use the term to scare and chastise those of us who want more progressive democratic social programs, like the ones that have worked in places like Norway and Sweden. Conservatives call progressives "sissies" or "crazy" and rally against them, saying they don't know what they're doing, when in reality, today's progressive communities and nations are fighting for a just, better world.

The proliferation of conservative religion, xenophobia, homophobia, racism, blind nationalism, misogyny and sexism, and the refusal of services and rights to the most at-need populations is not only disheartening but scary. I think about all of the politicians and leaders who have come and gone, the parties that have shot up and disappeared, and the struggle that continues for so many of us, and it all seems like one tired old game.

I pity the people who have never reconsidered what they've been taught, to understand the effects of their upbringing, schooling, and even workplace. Society must work to develop an open-minded, questioning habit; everyone should take a minute (or many) to reevaluate old anecdotes, beliefs, and concepts—whether in regards to social decorum or our own prejudices—to reach an enlightened state in which helping others, not hurting them, is the end goal.

I know it's hard. For a man of my age and experience, I find that the noise of everyday life can be overwhelming, with the howls of "fake news" from the right and the blatant lies on TV, online, or in print. People must become their own fact checkers, their own educators, separating advertisements, infotainment, and political propaganda from the simple truth, which is out there if they are willing to put in just a small amount of effort to discover it. Listening to publicly funded radio, watching a TED presentation online, or reading an unbiased newspaper can do wonders for one's education and understanding of what's really going on today.

I tend to proselytize on these subjects, but only because I believe there is so much at stake. I, of course, don't have all the answers, maybe no one does, but I've found that empathy and compassion—for each other, for the earth, for animals—goes a long way. Small contributions to help each other can have lasting effects, which I have seen proven repeatedly. As I've gotten older, I have been pleased to have the ability to help others as well, knowing that without the assistance that I received from friends, family, and strangers alike, I would have never succeeded.

It doesn't have to be a grand gesture either—the little things count just as much. For example, in 1988, a dear friend of mine who I knew from when I went to the Technical University, Cetin Saman, tragically died in a plane crash in Turkey. Cetin was a highly intelligent, excellent engineer. There wasn't a machine he couldn't figure out how to build, normally just by watching it in action, and after graduation he did well for himself by developing machinery that automated the production of brake lines. Most importantly, he was a great guy, honest, friendly, and always willing to help someone out in need—a real angel.

I flew back for the funeral, and though I wish it had been for a happier occasion, I had the chance to see family and old friends. I talked with Cetin's wife, Sema, about their son, Bora, who was friends with my son, Cenk. Nukhet and I had started taking the children back to Turkey every summer, and Cenk and Bora had developed a close relationship, almost like brothers. Bora felt like a son to me as well, and with his father gone I was concerned about his well-being, as I knew what it was like growing up without a dad. His mother was worried about him too, uncertain what he would do going forward, feeling that with Cetin gone, Bora would become rudderless.

"Say no more," I told her. "Why not have him come to the US and learn English? He can live with us in New Jersey and go to Rutgers. We'll take good care of him."

After I left, Sema told Bora about my suggestion. I hoped he would jump at my offer, but he was hesitant at first. He wanted to stay with his mother, be near his friends and the life that he was familiar with, but after talking it over with his mom, Cenk, and me, he decided it was an opportunity he couldn't pass up.

Cenk was happy to have his friend nearby, and Nukhet

and I enjoyed having Bora stay with us. He confided in me regularly, and I tried to give him the best advice I could. Years later he would tell me that not only did I help him learn English, but also about the American way of life, for which he was grateful.

After he finished school, he ended up returning to Turkey and entering his father's line of work, eventually starting his own brake-line tubing company. Early on, however, he ran into a number of snags, which led him into a desperate situation, both financially and mentally. He asked for my advice, and I flew to Istanbul the next day to help him figure out how to get out of the rut he was stuck in. We went over his finances, discussed the best way to run the business, and we got things back on track.

Today, his company produces some of the highest quality brake-line tubing ever made, exporting about $25-million worth of the product every year and employing 150 people. He told me that if it weren't for me offering him a place to stay in the US and for having suggested to his mother that he come live with us, he would have never gotten to this point—just a small amount of help can make the biggest difference in someone's life in the long run.

In return, he's helping others, not only through the products he makes, but also through the jobs he provides. I am as proud of Bora as I am of my own children, and I visit him whenever I go to Turkey. Once he said to me, "Whether you like or not, you are stuck with me because you are my father now," which I found touching beyond belief. He still calls me "father" and Nukhet "mother."

There may be nothing more life affirming than to see people I've helped go on to succeed and do important work—and I'm pleased that Bora's not the only one.

Right around when I sold my last commercial property, I received an email from a man named Mehmet Okur who used to work in my factory in Turkey. He had been an ambitious self-starter, working at the factory during the day and going to engineering school at night. He wrote me to ask if we could get together when I was in Turkey, and I of course obliged, always enjoying the chance to reconnect with people from my past.

When I met with him, however, I wasn't expecting an outpouring of appreciation. Mehmet told me all about how his life had progressed since working for me, and how he counted the years under my advisement as some of the most crucial. He believed I had helped him become a good engineer, and even a good person, so he says. Like many of the other Turkish engineers and manufacturers in the '70s, Mehmet had an innovative approach to production. He took an idea that he had developed in my factory, building circular vibrators, and ran with it later on, leading to his current success. Today he runs several factories of various kinds, mostly labeling bottles and other glass and plastic products—all told, his companies are worth a couple hundred million dollars.

In Turkey, he invited Nukhet and I to his house for dinner, and we enjoyed an excellent time together, talking about the many things that had happened to both of us since I left the country in 1978. He also insisted that I come meet up with him and a few of the other men who I had worked with back then. One of them—who had been a welder but also attended school at night—became one of the largest cement factory machinery producers in Turkey, building huge pieces of equipment. Today he exports products all over the world.

Just like Mehmet, he was happy to see me, and I felt a swell of emotion when he told me how much he and the others at the factory had learned from me and appreciated my work. He thanked me profusely. They also talked about other employees who had cut their teeth in my factory and then gone on to produce their own products and machinery, all of whom believed that part of their success came from working for me. It seemed that, in retrospect, much of my hope to help Turkish industry, and the people of Turkey, had indirectly come to fruition.

When we support others, we receive support in return, but most importantly it's an opportunity to create a better place that we can all be proud of. I believe helping others, and of course receiving help from others, has contributed to my success and longevity, and in this process I've garnered many lasting relationships and friendships that have enriched my life and made it one worth living to its fullest.

All the way back in 1968, when I moved to Istanbul after my military service, a group of friends and I started a monthly get-together that turned into such a large affair—almost twenty-five or thirty families meeting up the first Friday of every month—that I suggested we find a more permanent place to host our gatherings. Up until then we would meet at each other's houses, but this started becoming difficult due to the amount of people in our growing families.

Dogan and Cenk Uygur (son), pictured at a beach outside of Instanbul, Turkey, 1976.

We decided to buy a plot of land outside of Istanbul, overlooking the Black Sea, where we could all build small summer homes. The idea took off, and before I knew it we were spending many weekends and holidays there among our closest friends. We called the group ITU-MAK61, which stood for the Technical University of Istanbul mechanical engineers, graduating class of '61, which was how most of us had first met.

It was great—an opportunity for us all to reconnect every year, especially after I had moved to the US. It grounded me, keeping me in touch with my friends and my roots in Turkey. I unfortunately had to sell the house in the early 2000s, but I'm still in contact with all of those families. Whenever Nukhet and I go Turkey, we get together. In fact, Bora sometimes joins us, and he'll typically send his driver to pick us up at the airport—a real treat and something I would have never expected in a million years.

Having lived in Turkey and the US, I have friends in both countries, and though I spend most of my time in America, Nukhet and I have an apartment in Turkey, so we go there for a few months every year to visit. I keep in touch with friends from work, the Rotary Club, and the University of Maryland, and I see Bob Madden regularly. I have even stayed in touch with Serbulent Bingol, my former professor and the VP of Pasabahce Cam who helped me long ago. In 1974, he also helped me get into the Karaköy Rotary Club of Istanbul. He unfortunately passed away in the mid-2000s.

Maintaining such relationships is important. Not only does that type of social capital come in handy when trying to achieve goals, ask for advice, or get things done, but long, solid friendships provide so much more. Many of my friendships go back fifty to sixty years, and I value them as the greatest of treasures. The secret to these long-lasting and pleasant relationships is accepting others for who they are. People often get so wrapped up in who's "right" and who's "wrong," who won or lost an argument, but that's no way to go through life, especially when it comes to those who we hold dear.

Friendship is all about mutual support, not judging others for their shortcomings, but, instead, helping them overcome them if possible. Of course, there's no need to be forceful. Friends are critical to a fulfilling life, so I've tried to never scare anyone away with an overbearing, know-it-all attitude. Whenever I'm trying to get a point across or give some advice, I make sure to do so with a smile—encouraging my friends, not chastising them. I also make sure to listen to them, realizing that I'm not always right, and that people's thoughts, feelings, and beliefs, including my own, progress and change. Related, it's also important to gain younger friends who can provide insight and information that I may not have received otherwise—it keeps me on my toes, not to mention young at heart.

And though my friends have played an enormous role in my life, especially as I've gotten older, nothing has made me happier than my children and grandchildren, who I consider my greatest achievement above all else. All the jobs I've had, businesses I've ran, and money I've made can't hold a candle to the pride I have in my kids and their kids. They've all accomplished so much, and in them, I see many of the lessons that I have learned and passed down come to life in their efforts.

The biggest one is the pursuit of education. While raising Cenk and Sedef, I constantly stressed how important it was for them to do well in school and go to college, explaining how a college education was so pivotal in my life and their uncle's. Though Ihsan and I were the first in our family to go to college, today all of our extended family's children attend, both in the US and in Turkey.

Nukhet and I always tried to set a good example for Cenk and Sedef, and aside from encouraging them, we never preached to them or their children, telling them what to do or not to do with their lives. We made positive decisions when it came to food and exercise, and we never drank to excess or smoked, trying to show them that a healthy body creates a healthy mind. We talked about our views on religion openly and never forced our children to read the Quran or any other religious book. We told them it was up to them to make their own decisions about their beliefs and how they wanted to live.

I hoped for them both to be well-rounded, intelligent people, to live up to the Uygur name and be a force for good. Every Sunday, we would all sit around together and discuss stories from the *New York Times*, which Sedef has told me is one of her fondest memories of growing up. We talked about politics, history, art, literature—all the subjects I learned about over the years, those that I hadn't had access to in my youngest days in Kilis. I wanted my children to be educated, to succeed.

To that end, I was ecstatic when we sent Cenk off to college in Philadelphia, where he received his undergraduate degree at Wharton. When he finished, I suggested he go one step further and apply to graduate school. He really outdid himself, however, by going to Columbia Law, from which he graduated with honors. Nukhet and I were thrilled when he secured a position at a major law firm in DC. We were then equally astonished when, a mere eight months later, he told us he was leaving the practice to start a public access TV show.

"What the hell is a public access TV show?" I asked Nukhet.

The show didn't pan out as expected, and Cenk ended up back in New Jersey. I couldn't for the life of me understand what he was doing, but the more we talked about it, the more I relented. He had a vision, a foolish plan not unlike many of those I had when I was his age, and he wanted to follow it all the way through. He told me about a new TV station in Miami that was hiring reporters, and though he had little experience, I told him he needed to go. I let him borrow some money and said, "Don't come back until you get in."

Of course it wasn't that easy, but he worked his way into the station, first in sales, then in the newsroom, and he eventually went out on his own, moving to LA to develop a radio show, then an online news program— *The Young Turks.* I had the same attitude at Cenk's age, taking risks, seizing opportunities, and believing in myself. Just as the entrepreneurial spirit ran strong in me, and in Nukhet, it ran strong in Cenk as well. That one program morphed into the TYT network, which now has over sixteen million subscribers and ten billion lifetime views.

Through Cenk's TV show and media company, he's gotten to interview thousands of newsmakers, including top political figures from around the world. He even introduced me to Vice President Al Gore, who was wonderfully engaging, friendly, and gracious enough to correspond with me a number of times throughout the years. I cherish his letters just as I do my invitation from the White House and the time I shook Kennedy's hand.

Cenk also anchored on MSNBC and Current TV,

but TYT has always remained his main passion and commitment, aside from his wife, Wendy, whom he met when he moved to LA, and whom we all absolutely adore. Together, they have two wonderful children, Prometheus and Joy, who remind me of the best days of our early family life.

My daughter, Sedef, has amazed me too. After graduating from the Fashion Institute of Technology with a degree in Fashion Buying and Merchandising, she went on to raise a family with her husband, Mehmet, in Istanbul, Turkey. Mehmet, who is currently a professor at Özyeğin University in Istanbul, was also a successful executive at Sabanci Holding, one of the largest conglomerates in Turkey.

When her son Hasan started college, Sedef moved back to New Jersey and returned to school, where she received a Bachelor of Arts in Art History at Rutgers University. From there, her love of art just wouldn't let her stop, and she's currently pursuing her doctorate in Architectural History at New Jersey Institute of Technology. How she has found the time, I don't know. I believe Nukhet and I were good influences on Sedef; she saw how hard her mother and father worked to get to where we are, and then she followed in our footsteps. Just as I see myself in Cenk, I see myself in her as well, with her tireless work effort and her focus on family. I'm sure her interest in art, design, and fashion came from Nukhet, and I'm in awe of how she has approached her education with such gusto.

From left: Dogan Uygur, his wife, and his 4 grandchildren.

In 2002, I helped Sedef and Mehmet buy and manage a two-story, 18,000-square-foot office building while they still lived in Turkey. After moving back to the states for her sons' education, Sedef took over the building's day-to-day operations, but to this day, she still calls me regularly to ask for advice. She always says, "I am an Art Historian. Everything I know about managing a building, I learned from my father."

I still go to the building and help her out from time to time, so I guess I'm not fully "out" of the real estate game. When I'm there, it makes me so proud to receive positive feedback from her tenants, knowing that she's put all my advice to such good use. I have no doubt that her work ethic and lifestyle greatly influenced her two children, my grandsons, Hasan and Murat Piker, who have grown into fine young men, both graduating from Rutgers University and setting off on their own careers and aspirations.

My older grandson, Hasan, went to work for Cenk, continuing the long tradition of our family members helping each other. Hasan learned the ins and outs of a modern news network, from video production to on-air reporting, and worked for a number of departments. He hosts his own show on the TYT network called *The Breakdown*, in which he discusses the day's news in an up-to-date, fast-paced segment. He's amassed over 500 million reviews of his videos and influenced a whole generation of young people across the world. My other grandson, Murat, was always science-minded and received a degree in mechanical and aerospace engineering—I like to think I had some influence there, though aerospace engineering is far beyond me. Today, Murat works for Boeing in Los Angeles, where he helps send satellites and spaceships off into the sky. Both his and Hasan's success fills me with happiness; I am a proud grandfather.

In my long life, I've never had any major, lasting regrets. I never cheated anyone or knowingly hurt others. I worked hard and passed my values on to my children and to their children, supporting my family as my family supported me. Though the American Dream may feel out of reach for so many today, I'm thankful for my ability to have attained it in my lifetime. Putting family first, working hard, getting an education, building a business, maintaining an entrepreneurial spirit, helping others— these were the keys to my achievements, and they can lead to success today for a younger generation, despite the challenges faced.

It's been quite the ride, starting with very little in my hometown, coming to America, getting my degrees, running a factory, buying buildings, living through political and social change—resilience has been essential. I've never given up, no matter what. There are always a thousand excuses that can stand in the way of success, but there are also a thousand ways to get around those excuses and those barriers to reach one's dreams. It can be a hard road, but the end destination is worth it.

I may have slowed down a bit here in my eighties, but I don't mind. It's enough for me to see my children and grandchildren thriving and succeeding. Sometimes at night, I walk out into my backyard in Freehold, New Jersey, and I look up at the sky, seeing the same vast sea of stars and bright yellow moon that I looked up at as a young boy on a balcony in a small Turkish town. I think about how somewhere out there, there's a satellite that one of my grandson's worked on and shot into orbit, an idea that I wouldn't have been able to fathom when I was a child, and I smile knowing that when I someday leave this world, I'll do so at peace, over a life well lived.

Conclusion

WE LIVE IN COMPLEX, DIFFICULT times, at home here in the US and abroad. Young people face challenges that I didn't have to contend with, as they're coming of age in a place that, in many ways, is starting to feel less democratic at every turn. But I did have to overcome many obstacles of my own due to where and when I was born and the challenges inherent in that era and the others I've lived through. The lessons illustrated by my life's story, however, are evergreen, applicable no matter one's place of birth or circumstances; I truly believe this, as I have seen these lessons at work not just in my life but in others'.

I cannot stress enough the importance of family, friends, and a strong community—the bedrock to all of my success. We can't decide to whom we are born or where, and families can certainly be challenging, but if we listen to one another and support each other, that natural bond deepens and grows. We can also decide to surround ourselves with other positive influences and people, developing our own communities. Many find these new groups of mutual support once they head off to college, an important aspect of the educational experience, though not the only one.

Education should be seen as a guiding light throughout

life, not just when we're children, teenagers, or in our early twenties. As we learn, we grow, which helps us succeed in all our endeavors. Understanding other people's points of view teaches us empathy and provides us with the knowledge that we are all in this together, in one way or another. As we age, education also helps us question our assumptions and long-held beliefs, leading to a richer, more informed life. We are taught so many things as children that are either misinformed or incorrect; it's imperative to seek out the truth as we get older. And it's easier than ever today—if only the internet had existed when I was a boy in Kilis.

Educational attainment tends to build self-confidence, which is essential to taking risks and seizing opportunities. We can sit around timidly and do nothing with our lives out of fear of failure—or on the advice of others to follow the crowd—but by doing so, we miss out while the world passes us by. Sometimes it's necessary to fully throw one's self into something even if the outcome is uncertain. Success doesn't come by playing it safe, and unless we're willing to take chances, we'll never know what could have been.

I took many chances in my life and made the best of all the opportunities that presented themselves, including marrying Nukhet. Life truly is better when it is spent with others, the people we love and trust. The relationship between life partners is so very unique and so very precious that we do ourselves a disservice by not seeking it out. If it weren't for Nukhet, there are so many things that I wouldn't have been able to do, and I am forever indebted to her. She fully supported every one of my entrepreneurial decisions, even when others thought they were ridiculous, and I knew I couldn't let her down. Without her, I would have never been able to open my own business in Turkey or enter real estate in the US, and my life would be much different indeed.

Dogan's family; his children, and grandchildren. Pictured top left:Nukhet, Dogan, Cenk, Murat, Sedef, Hasan, and Mehmet. Pictured bottom row from left: Promethius Maximus, Joy Helena, and Wendy.

Starting companies was one of my most gratifying experiences. Not only did I enjoy learning about various industries and businesses, but there is also an incomparable sense of pride and accomplishment in creating a successful venture—being one's own boss pays off too, both financially and personally. It's not without its own headaches, learning curves, and set-backs, but in the end it's all worth it. That said, simply having an entrepreneurial mindset and a relentless attitude helps in any type of professional setting, as it forces one to think outside of the box, find creative solutions, and work hard.

Much of my success has been due to putting in the hours when others couldn't, wouldn't, or didn't want to. I may have pushed it too much, reaching the verge of burning out, but in all, my work ethic was a virtue. In many ways I owe that to my mother, forcing me out to those plots of land first thing every morning when I was a boy. The values she instilled in me at a young age paved the way for my endurance, strength, and perseverance in both my education and working life, and when I experienced failures, I knew I could move forward.

Still, overcoming failure isn't ever easy. Without failing once in a while, though, we never learn some of life's most important lessons, such as the virtues of humility and persistence. Things don't always work out as planned, and though I've been fortunate, I had to make some detours to get to where I am. When nothing's working, we may have to change course, but we can never give up. We need to figure out how to take the next step, climb out of the hole we have found ourselves in, and get resituated on the path toward success and personal and professional fulfillment.

Finding fulfillment, a sense of contentment, is at the heart of all these lessons, and I'm happy to say that for me it all comes back to family. Even if I could have picked all the grapes and olives in Turkey, acted in the biggest Hollywood movies, sold all the pots and pans in New

Jersey, written the greatest poems of all time, produced all the electromagnetic vibrating feeders ever, or rented out all the commercial real estate across the US, none of it would be worth it without family and friends to share in my success. I know I have lived a charmed life by the people that surround me—my wife, my children, my grandchildren, and my closest friends and relatives. In them, I find joy and enlightenment, happiness and a sense of peace.

And I hope this book has brought readers joy and enlightenment as well, along with a good dose of entertainment, providing advice that can be used to make our individual lives and collective lives better. If we live honestly, foster genuine friendships and relationships, and extend a helping hand when others need it, whenever possible, then we can make this world a better place. Furthermore, if we take our education seriously, learn from our mistakes, listen to and care for one another, and endure in the face of hardship, we will be unstoppable.

About the Author

DOGAN UYGUR IS AN ENGINEER, entrepreneur, and writer. Born and raised in southern Turkey, he attended college in Istanbul before moving to the US for graduate school in 1961. He has started and run businesses both in Turkey and America, including *Enternasyonal Makina Sanayi*, a company that was at the forefront of Turkish machine manufacturing during the 1970s. After escaping political upheaval in Turkey in 1978, he returned to the US, where he worked in commercial real estate for nearly thirty years. Today, he lives in Freehold, New Jersey, with his wife, Nukhet.